ALL I
WORDS
HAVE
HOLES
IN THEM

simple daily meditations
GINNY WILDER

Church Publishing
NEW YORK

This book is dedicated to my Mom and Dad,
Ginga and John Wilder. Thank you for teaching me
at a very young age that God is indeed everywhere,
in the stories that we share and in the prayers
that we pray. You both taught me that the holes
in our words weren't something to be fixed
but rather something to be explored.

Copyright © 2017 by Ginny Wilder

Church Publishing
19 East 34th Street
New York, NY 10016
www.churchpublishing.org

Cover design by Paul Soupiset
Interior design and typesetting by Beth Oberholtzer Design

A record of this book is available from the Library of Congress.

ISBN-13: 978-0-8192-3382-0 (pbk.)
ISBN-13: 978-0-8192-3383-7 (ebook)

Printed in the United States of America

CONTENTS

INTRODUCTION

All my words have holes in them. When experiencing something so intimate or so big or beyond my ability to grasp and respond, I find the words I use to describe or make sense of the moment fail, epically. No matter how many words I use to try and articulate, explain, give thanks, or just respond, I feel like my words fail to fully hold the emotion of the moment. These holes leave room for the Holy. These holes leave room for the mystery. These holes leave room for the consideration that God—the love of God, the ways of God—is beyond our understanding and our ability to fully comprehend . . . and that is okay.

How one experiences God is unique and different, and no singular experience is perfect or complete. The holes in our words when we pray leave room for another person's response and prayer, too. Connecting, recollecting, sharing our own unique and different relationships with God helps to manifest the Kingdom of God here, on earth, and now, in our time. The holes in our words help make that possible. No one response is complete or perfect but they are all "holy."

What you hold in your hands is a collection of "holy" moments captured in prayers, stories, reflections, and poems that tries to use words to illuminate the extraordinary among the ordinary—in our breathing, remembering, praying, releasing, and reconciling.

All my words have holes in them and I am okay with that.

BREATHING

Life begins with breath so, in a sense, we begin
with breathing. Instinctive, life-giving, purposeful, second
nature, the process to keep us moving, living, hoping, and
praying is wired in the muscles that allow us to inhale and
exhale and take a breath.

God breathed over creation. God breathes us into life. The
life that is in your body and in your soul is rooted in the act
of Creation; today is a new day waiting for you to breathe life
into the world around you.

Breathing—taking a pause, a moment before beginning a
new day or before closing your eyes at the end of the day—
offers us a place to land in the space between inhale and
exhale. I am guilty of blowing right through that pause in
order to get to the next thing on my to-do list, on my agenda,
to my next thought. I am guilty of ignoring the natural spaces
and places and pauses because sometimes "to stop" is harder
than "to start."

Breathing, mindful and intentional, can become prayer.
Breathing gives us voice to speak and to pray. Breathing is
the beginning of creation and creating. Through the breath of
God, we have life within us. What we do today will be fueled by
breath and blood and all throughout the day we are given nat-
ural pauses to inhale, give thanks, exhale and continue to move
and live and have our being. It starts with breath.

Quitting

She took a long drag off her Salem Lights cigarette and blew smoke rings into the rainy and dreariness of the afternoon. It had been years since my lips curled around the butt of a smoke, but I caught myself breathing in with her and then breathing out with her, trying to remember the heat of fire, the cool of menthol, the pause between breaths to hold on just a little longer before letting it all go.

She looked at me, right at me. Who does that in this day and age? We look at our watches, our smart phones, our laptops, doing everything in our power not to connect with anyone. Only anythings. She looked right at me and caught me looking at her. She inhaled again. I did too. She exhaled. I did too. And then she did the unthinkable: she talked to me.

"Do you want one?"

Yes, for the love of God, I want the whole pack. That's what I was thinking anyway. Instead I replied, "No thank you, I quit."

"Huh. You could have fooled me."

I was a little offended. It had been four years, seven months, and twenty-one days since my last cigarette. I thought I had successfully quit smoking.

"You know, the funny thing about the word 'quit' is that it's a place holder, a verb that's vamping until it's ready. You can only quit for so long before you begin something else."

I looked up from my smartphone and made eye contact with the smoking stranger. Sensing permission had been granted, she continued to speak.

"I mean, think about it. We quit school. We quit jobs. We quit going to church. We quit exercising. We quit drinking. The physical act of quitting takes place but our emotional connection, our mental connection—those things don't quit. I once quit dating someone, but it took me years to move beyond the quitting into the living." She took another long drag causing the cherry to glow orange and red while leaving a trail of smoke dancing on the end of her dazzling white cigarette. "I swear one day I'm going to not smoke. I'm not going to quit, I am just not going to smoke. Quitting leaves room to begin again."

Quitting leaves room to begin again.

I turned the phrase over and over in my mind as I waited for the trolley to come. She had long since snuffed out her cigarette and returned to what I believe was her place of work. I was left to inhale the lingering smoke and think about all the things I had quit. There was a list—which took me by surprise. I quit practicing the piano. I quit taking time each day to pray or meditate. I quit rinsing out the recyclables before putting them in the container. I quit telling the whole truth sometimes. I quit taking in the beauty around me, seeing the seasons as they unfolded with each passing day. I quit making time for the things that brought me joy. The list went on and on. When I stepped off the trolley twenty minutes later, I felt defeated. I was alive, but I was barely breathing, barely living.

Quitting leaves room to begin again.

I needed to begin something again. Maybe I needed to revisit my list of quits and see if there were any "begin agains" there.

I slipped the key into the door, turned the handle, and I entered my own little sanctuary, covered and comforted by all my stuff. Suddenly, none of it felt so comforting. I was second guessing all the quits it took for me to get here. What was the price of this life? What had it cost me along the way?

Damn that smoking stranger.

I sat down on the couch and had a reckoning with myself. I had spent so much time quitting this and quitting that, becoming laser-like in my focus and determination that I quit everything else that didn't fit into this one perfect, neat, and lonely life. I was shaking, but I needed to say it out loud, so my ears could hear it in my own voice, "I quit quitting and I begin beginning." There was no applause or sweeping orchestra music. The occasion was marked only by a neighbor slamming his door as he left for his evening shift at the hospital. I sat on the couch and let the dust of my proclamation settle, and as the light of the day gave way to the light of the evening, I called my brother. I just needed to hear his voice. It had been so long. In the list of things I had quit, I realized my family was one I quit a while ago. One ring. Two rings. Three rings.

"Hello?"

"Hey, it's me." I lingered for a moment.

Before I could speak he said, "Yes, I know it's you. Your name popped up on my phone. What's up?"

I breathed in, longing to feel the burn of smoke, but instead, I felt the fire of life begin to catch. "I was wondering if you wanted to get some dinner? I could really use the company tonight. It has been a weird day, but I think I am beginning to see the light."

Those who try to make their life secure will lose it, but those who lose their life will keep it. (Luke 17:33)

Some Questions for Your Consideration

1. The smoking stranger became an unexpected prophet for the author. Who, in your own life, has been an unexpected prophet?

2. If you looked over your life for the past five years, have you done more quitting or more beginning?

3. What have you gained by quitting? What have you given up by beginning?

4. What have you gained by beginning? What have you given up by quitting?

5. You get one phone call in that moment of need and I wonder: who are you going to call and why?

Lord, we give you thanks for the unexpected prophets that we encounter along the way. Help us to hear them, hear you in them, and help us to let go and to hold on, to quit and begin, to become, even when it is painful, and to become again, to begin again. Amen.

Gently She Breathes

Gently she breathes.
A rhythm, a call and response
In and out
Inhale, Exhale
I place my hand to feel the rise and fall
There are bones underneath this skin,
bones that have been here for a long, long time.
The room is dark, afternoon light is not generous to this
    space
Gently she breathes
A rhythm, a call and response
labored, tired
like the body knows these moments are fleeting
the mind has already gone, the spirit is just here
turning off the lights, one by one until the only light left

is what comes through the slots of the blinds pulled shut.
Soon evening will be settling in.
Gently she breathes
A rhythm, a call and response
It is okay, I say
Your work here is done
You have said all your prayers
you have shared all the stories
We will miss you sweet friend
We already do.
Gently she lets go
The drum skips a beat
Shadows lengthen
a call and response.
Welcome home.

What they don't prepare us for in seminary is how to grieve and mourn the loss of our parishioners. Writing has helped me but I feel the loss deeply. So do your priests, pastors, and ministers.

Our Bag of Truth

If I hold my breath just long enough, sometimes I can escape the horror of speaking my truth. Sometimes our truth is a burden to us, to those around us, to those we don't even know. Our truth can be understood as a basket, a grocery cart, a shoulder bag, a vessel that holds things—tiny objects, huge boulders, a trinket, a memory, a favorite song, a missed opportunity, things we have done and left undone; everything stored neatly or shoved into that vessel we call truth that we carry with us, everywhere we go. Sometimes we have to set the bag down and dig deep into the darkness, searching for the one item that always seems to be buried underneath mountains of randomness and brokenness that we carry as a part of our truth. We shake the bag, we dive our hands into the clutter, and we search through the random and discarded bits of unfinished items, words we shouldn't have said, words we should have said; sometimes we get lucky and we find what we are looking for. We bring it out into the light of day. After we are through with it, we place it right back into the mixed bag of truth and we carry it. Carry it. Carry it on our shoulders, on our backs, in our hands.

Our truth is filled with so much. Our experiences, our expectations, our disappointments, our hopes. Our hearts—even when our hearts have been broken. We carry the wounds and the scars and the lessons learned. This truth is as much a part of who we are as the color of our eyes, the blood in our veins, the hair on our heads. We weren't born with those scars, but we wear them like badges of courage. Some of us draw life from them the same way we draw life from the air that we breathe.

I hold my breath, sometimes, long enough to escape the discomfort of saying what I feel, what I think, what I want, what I need, what I'm upset about. The words and thoughts never make it beyond my soft palate, but I still harbor them, in my bag of truth. The unsaid words add weight to the pile, the mound, the heap that is my truth. The emotion tied to those words has a weight of its own. The only thing I have gained by not saying what I need to say is more weight, more clutter, more guilt for feeling what I feel and for not saying what I needed to say.

Weighted down, hands full, heart empty, distracted by wondering how absurd I look dragging my bag of truth around, I make excuses so as not to be seen in public because I know the moment I go out into the world my bag of truth might all come spilling out and the mess it will make will be more than I can handle. Especially now. We are in the season of hoping and waiting—but most everywhere else in our lives, we are in the season of counting down—this many months until our vacation, this many weeks until school begins or ends, this many days until the weekend, this many hours until we can go home, and this many minutes before the coffee is ready. All this counting down keeps me busy and occupied. All this counting down keeps me from working through my bag of truth.

"The beginning of the good news of Jesus Christ, the Son of God." That is how the Gospel of Mark begins. He lets us in on the true identity of Christ right from the very start. We don't have to figure it out for ourselves, we don't have to wait for the angel to appear to Mary, we don't have to wait for the wise men, and we don't have to wait for Herod to come after the Christ Child. Mark tells us from the very beginning and then, rather than writing about the birth of Jesus, he does something incredibly beautiful: he tells the deeper truth, the deeper story. Mark highlights the words of the prophet Isaiah.

See, I am sending my messenger ahead of you,
    who will prepare your way;
the voice of one crying out in the wilderness:
    "Prepare the way of the Lord."

Enter John the Baptist in all his funky glory, in all his questionable fashion sense, in all his odd diet of locust and honey, and all his heart set on one task: to prepare the way of the Lord.

John the Baptist visited me this week in my prayer time. I was sitting at my desk reading Mark's words and shaking my head because I was so distracted by my bag of truth, which was resting at the corner of my desk. I knew what was in that bag. I placed every object inside that cluttered heaping mess. There were tendrils of guilt, shame, doubt, worry, hope, love, joy, wonder, and awe tied to most every thing that was part of my truth, and the tangled mess kept growing, getting bigger, to the point where I didn't know if I could carry it around anymore.

John, gruff and unkempt, showed up in my heart. I paused long in my prayer time to sit with this man who at once scares me and comforts me. I asked him, "How? How can I prepare the way of the Lord? I barely have enough energy to prepare my breakfast some days, let alone preparing the way of the Lord. How can I watch and wait with hope?"

He seemed to hear me, but he said nothing. In fact, he didn't say anything the whole time. He just waited, with me, in that space and every once in a while he glanced over at my bag of truth and then looked back at me. And waited.

Prepare the way of the Lord, make his paths straight.
Every valley shall be lifted up,
and every mountain and hill be made low;
the uneven ground shall become level,
and the rough places a plain.

John, in his silence, was letting me know that the road to my heart was anything but straight, lifted up, level, or plain. It is a mountain of brokenness that needs to be dealt with. That was my truth.

When John shows up in the Gospel story, he acts like a clearing house, creating a touching place to expose our wounds and truth and hurts and the ways we have wounded and hurt others. A place to tell our story, tell our truth, and leave behind what is no longer ours to carry. John meets us there, surrounded by what we have unpacked from our bag of truth. He meets us with water: to cleanse us, to clean our wounds, and to clear space in our lives that lets the path to our hearts—to our own manger where we long to hold the Christ child—become straighter, lower, more level, more plain. We confess. We offer our broken bits, our messy bits, our disappointed bits, our hurt bits, our shame, our guilt, our mistakes, our missed opportunities, the words we should have said, the words we shouldn't have said, the things we have done, and the things we have left undone. John offers us water and a chance to be forgiven as we repent of each of these. The repenting is where we truly let these items go. I can unpack every truth, show them to John, even have them washed in water, but if I don't say, I'm sorry, or please forgive me, then I am just putting these newly washed bits of truth right back in my bag and continuing to walk down a very difficult road, weighted down.

Some of the items in my bag of truth have been washed and washed and washed over many years, but the words I need to say in order to truly be relieved of them haven't come. I haven't had the strength to say those words . . . yet. One day, I will be able to speak out loud to the strange, hairy visitor. One day I will be ready to say what I need to say in order to leave these things behind. John takes them, washes them in water, pats them dry, and hands them back to me. I put them right back in my bag of truth. I want to say he smiles. I want to say that I feel relieved just by showing John some of my deepest hurts. But when the weight lands back on my shoulder, on my back, the relief is not there. The relief I am looking for comes only in the form of confessing and repenting. To prepare the way of the Lord is to confess and repent.

Preparing the way of the Lord begins with being open and honest and looking into our history, our own bags of truth, and seeing what we continue to carry that clutters our hands and hearts and prevents us from being able to hold onto the gift of life, the gift of salvation, the gift of redemption, the gift of Jesus Christ.

Prepare the way of the Lord.

What do we have in our hearts that may block us, or make the journey more difficult? We want relief. I want relief. I need to hand these heavy bits of my truth over to the one who can redeem me. For good. By confessing and repenting.

I'm working on that. That is my truth.

Amen.

The beginning of the good news of Jesus Christ,
    the Son of God.
As it is written in the prophet Isaiah,
"See, I am sending my messenger ahead of you,
who will prepare your way;
the voice of one crying out in the wilderness:
'Prepare the way of the Lord,
make his paths straight,"'

John the baptizer appeared in the wilderness, proclaiming a baptism of repentance for the forgiveness of sins. And people from the whole Judean countryside and all the people of Jerusalem were going out to him, and were baptized by him in the river Jordan, confessing their sins. Now John was clothed with camel's hair, with a leather belt around his waist, and he ate locusts and wild honey. He proclaimed, "The one who is more powerful than I is coming after me; I am not worthy to stoop down and untie the thong of his sandals. I have baptized you with water; but he will baptize you with the Holy Spirit." (Mark 1:1–8)

I Cannot on My Own

Long before Lent is over each year, I begin practicing the Exsultet, the Easter Proclamation sung on Holy Saturday at the beginning of the Easter Vigil, and I always feel like I am cheating a little bit by doing so. While my congregation is still out in the wilderness, still in the highs and lows of fasting, wondering, and praying, part of me is already living in Easter. The words that follow grew out of one such season.

This has been the strangest Lent I can remember.
I have managed to maintain my fasts—which is a
   miracle—
and I have been aware of the desire to break both of them
and instead of giving up, I give in, surrender to God,
remember that I am dust, full of imperfection
but still loved by our holy, loving God.

I hunger for the feeling of peace that comes
once I surrender
once I give in
once I remember time and time again
that I cannot do this on my own.
I cannot live this life on my own.
I cannot serve God on my own.
I cannot love my neighbors on my own.
I cannot be Christ to another on my own.

I need you.

I love you.

This is not a new revelation, but one that pops up from
    time to time—
I cannot fully love God without fully loving you.
And I take comfort in the understanding that I fail
all the time
but I am given the chance to try, try, try, try, try again.

And in that revelation, I realize that mini Easters happen
    all the time—even in Lent.

Some Questions for Your Consideration

1. Do you practice fasting during the season of Lent?
   Why or why not?

2. If yes, what have you learned through fasting?

3. If no, what do you think about fasting during Lent?

4. What is the strangest thing you have ever heard of
   someone (or maybe you) giving up or fasting from
   during Lent?

5. What do you think that fast allowed the person to
   gain during Lent?

My Wired and Wounded Soul

She waits for me in the corner
My little wooden friend
A wired and wounded soul
Who knows what my tears taste like

She hums along to any tune
She bends and she swoops
Like a bird on a branch
Waiting, watching
Until it is time to fly

I hold her close
To my heart, to my soul
I breathe into her
Stretch my hand across her familiar grain and grooves

I know her skin like I know my own
I know her exhales and her inhales
I know when I have ignored her for too long
And I know when she has had enough

Come sing to me, she whispers
Come let me add my own harmony
Come and tell me that story
That secret
That fear
I will hold it safely, I will tell no one

She is my beautiful beast
The one that has taken me places I could not go alone
And still she sits in the shadow, protected from the light
And she waits, and waits
Ready when I am
To sing our song.

Let everything that breathes praise the Lord!
Praise the Lord! (Psalm 150:6)

Held

There is a longing within that makes itself known in my prayer time. A deep yearning to be cradled, held, considered precious. This longing is not uncommon but uncomfortable because I would like to think that at my age, I am too grown up for such desires. This morning as my heart sighed and this longing emerged, I caught a glimpse of how this longing isn't a longing but a reality. I am cradled. I am held. I am considered precious by our God and the feeling was not a yearning but an understanding, a thank you, a recognition of a deeper connection. I rested there, lingered there, began my day from that space, that connection, that love.

REMEMBERING

I grew up sitting at the feet of some amazing storytellers in my family. After Sunday dinner dessert would be served, the true sweetness of the meal happened in hearing my grandmothers and my aunts and uncles and my parents share stories from their history, threads from their tapestries. Laughter mixed with real South Carolina Low Country sweet tea made from a sugar syrup was the champagne of these meals. The remembering of events, of people and places and things, and the sharing of these items infused my soul with a connection to my story and gave me a root into the many names that make up the genealogy of my family. Remembering opens up the portal from today into yesterday without any technology needed.

Remembering allows us to hold space for those who have gone before us too. Most of the stories around the dinner table on those Sunday afternoons were of people I would never get to meet, but in the words and expressions shared by my elders, they were as alive for me as if they were in the room with us. And the joy in the smiles of those telling the stories was real, deep, honest, and a gift to share.

Remembering with our souls and our hearts can sometimes be painful too. There are people I have lost in one fashion or another that my heart grieves and mourns, and when I remember them I am overwhelmed by sadness, by the void in my life that their larger-than-life presence used to fill. Even in my grief, however, I give thanks that the love we shared for each other was rich and full and a source of something I miss no matter how long it has been since they departed this world.

Remembering connects us in ways that are hard to describe with words, but our hearts know and understand. Remembering draws from us the ability to be both here and there at the same time, holding onto the love we miss and the life we have.

I Haven't Forgotten About You

I haven't forgotten about you.
I see you hanging out in the corner,
checking your watch
looking at your to do list.
I haven't forgotten about you at all.
Even though I tried, all day.
I know you are here, waiting as long as you need to.
Waiting until the right moment—the moment that is
    far beyond my understanding
to step in.
And when you do, you will offer relief to him.
You will leave us, those who stay behind,
to grapple with our own loss, our own pain, our own
    hurts.
You don't do much for us.
That is not in your job description.
You come to take/relieve the dying.
For them you are a blessing.
For us you are many things but a blessing is way down
    on the list of words we would use to describe you.

I haven't forgotten you.
I see traces of you on the walls,
on the e-mails that I send,
on the plans I make for the days to come.
Your fingerprints are all over them
in the disguise as back-up plans,
of just in case,
of please not today.
But when it is time,
no matter how many plans we have put in place,
we will still need to honor your role, your job,
and let him go with the same grace he has shown us,
Has offered us.
Has taught us.
He said he is ready. He has made his peace with the
    world, within himself, and with God.
But I pout, kick the floor and long to hold on as long
    as I can.
I know that this isn't helpful.
I know this isn't meet and right.
I know this isn't holy.
But this is how I feel.
I haven't forgotten about you
And I will never forget him. Amen.

The Hour of Our Birth

The hour of our birth
I was born at 11:11pm
In the eleventh month
Second child
First daughter

Only daughter.
The hour of our birth
I was born again
And again
And again
Still being born
When I had my first kiss
When I got my driver's license
When I yelled at God
And wondered out loud
Are you some kind of sick and twisted God?
The hour of our birth
I try to practice the art of living
And not so much the habits of dying
But some days—some days
Death sneaks up, taps me on the shoulder
And says, "Not today, but some day."
And then I wonder, will I have
Enough time, before My Time, to do
All that is on my to do list?
The hour of our birth
I was not born to make lists
Or to scratch things off my list
Or to live in the pain, struggle, anxiety
That a list often brings with it.
No, I was born, and born again, and born and born
    and born and born
To try and mess up
To love and have my heart broken
To try and mess up
To love and have my heart broken open
To try and try again

To understand that sticks and stones break bones
But words hurt most of all
To try and mess up and be forgiven
To love and have my heart skip a beat
To try and mess up and be okay with that
To love and have my heart searched and understood
To try and love
The hour of our birth
Rebirth
Reconciled
Reconnect
Revealed
Rejoice
Born.

Yes, I Remember

She said, "Remember that one time when we stole across
the lawn, down around the street corner, and up to the
place where we could see every star in heaven?"
"I do." That was my reply.

She said, "We tried to hold our breath long enough, just
long enough so that our very life, our exhales, wouldn't
block out the light of the stars."
"Yes, I remember," I said.

She said, "Dressed in layers, from our feet to our head,
mittens and scarves, mittens and scarves—clashing
colors and patterns. We didn't care back then if what we
wore matched."
"Yes, this I recall."

She said, "You were searching the sky for the one star that spoke your name, whispered it on the last days of winter, haunting the horizon, beckoning you to dance in the light, the ancient, ancient light."
"Yes, I remember."

She said, "You said you believed in a Creator that knew the colors and birthed them from within—you said you wish that our language could truly hold the essence of our emotions—that our modern language was a poor vessel for the way your heart felt when you gazed upon such openness, such wideness, such beauty."
"Yes, I remember all of this."

She said, "You said you hoped for a time in your own life when you could feel as free as light, as light as freedom, and as whole as the connection that bound you to the stars."
"Yes, I remember this as if it were yesterday."

She said, "You said, 'The only way any of this was possible is through a love that knows all the languages, all the feelings, all the hopes, all the dreams, and a love that knows my name.'"
"Yes, I remember."

She exhaled, "I do too; and it is a beautiful prayer."
Amen.

Tonight, step outside after the night has fallen where you live, stare up at the sky, focus on one star, and whisper your name. Whisper the name you were given at birth. Whisper all the names you have been called since your birth. Whisper the name you wish you had been called. Whisper all of these names and then listen to the world around you hold all of the names you have spoken.

Tell Me the Story

Tell me the story again, about how we met, almost by accident. You were standing in the aisle of the self-help section in the mall bookstore, and you were debating whether you should stop and get a coffee.

Tell me again, that story, the song that was playing—one of those lovely pieces from Bonnie Raitt's *Nick of Time*. A saxophone playing on the overhead speakers. The smell of sandalwood drifting from the candles two rows over.

Tell me that story again of how we met. You had given up everything, you thought. You did everything you thought you were supposed to do and you still didn't have any more answers than you did originally. I could tell that. It was written in your heart, all over your face, and in the three tattoos your sleeves covered.

Tell me again about that time we met. You were subconsciously twirling your hair around your finger, looking at the covers, the titles, the pictures, and the authors of a life and a confidence you longed to have. You thought about the journal, the one tucked in your bedside table, about the notes you had written to your younger self or your older self—you weren't quite sure which "you" you were writing to.

You had nodded your head like you had come to some kind of agreement, some kind of conclusion, some kind of answer. Yes, perhaps I will stop for a coffee and I will go home, but first I have to buy a book. Some answers written by someone I have never met. A guru in a pink button-down polo and a brighter-than-white smile, with perfect hair. Will it be a man? Will it be a woman? Does it really matter?

Tell me about the time we met in the self-help aisle, in the bookstore, in the mall that had recently seen two stores close, and one going out of business. Tell me about that story. Remember that story. About when we met, and you thought it was the first time. The fluorescent flickering light above your head weaving itself in and out of the saxophone drone, and you searching the covers for an answer to a question you didn't know how to ask. And you said, "God. I just need some help." Amen.

Some Questions for Your Consideration

1. Do you have any tattoos?
2. If yes, why? If no, why?
3. Has anyone ever stepped in while your were experiencing deep need and offered you the peace of God?
4. Have you ever been that person for another?
5. What do you think happened next in this story?

These Are My Tears

She asked, "Do you remember that one time when we ran down to the ocean in the middle of the night, in the middle of the summer? We stood out there for so long tracing the moon's journey across the sky."

"Yes," I said while trying to gather the heat of that summer night in my hands, recalling the warmth and the humidity, feeling it on my skin, in my lungs as I breathed in.

She said, "We stood there for what felt like hours trying to count the stars, getting lost in the vastness of the sky. I have never felt so small and so loved at the same time."
"Yes," I said, as I closed my eyes and saw the brilliant stars behind my eyelids. They were quite stunning and felt so close. "We held hands as we ran up to the sea."

She said, "We dipped our toes into the low tide rolling, rolling, rolling."
"Yes," I said. "I remember the salt, the water, the sand, all touching our feet at the same time and leaving behind a trace like a fingerprint, and I couldn't help but wonder how long the water had been there before it touched our skin."

"Do you remember how warm the water was?" she asked.
"Yes," I replied, as I reached down to my toes to touch the place where the sea touched me and instinctively I lifted my hand to my head and I traced the symbol of the cross on my forehead. Remember. Remember. Remember.

"We really are all connected," she said. "The stars, the water, the sand, the sky—we are all connected. Isn't that something?"
"Yes," I said. "How could I ever forget?" I stood there breathing in deeply and feeling myself wrapped in an embrace of a memory, a vow, a promise, and a covenant.

"Why are you weeping?" she asked.

"Sometimes when words fail, tears step in to give voice to what we feel. The language of tears is as ancient as the stars, the sea, the sky, and older than the story within our blood and bones. Sometimes the only response to this kind of love, the one that is always coming to us, seeking us, longing to reach out and leave the mark of water and remembrance upon our skin, is an equal response of water, mingled with salt and awe. These are my tears for the journey. These are my tears for the life. These are my tears for the love that knows no boundaries or barriers, and this is the only way I know how to say 'Thank you.'"

"Amen," she said as she took my hand in hers.
Amen.

For I am convinced that neither death, nor life, nor angels, nor rulers, nor things present, nor things to come, nor powers, nor height, nor depth, nor anything else in all creation, will be able to separate us from the love of God in Christ Jesus our Lord. (Romans 8:38–39)

The Farmer's Lament: A Different Take on Lamentations 1:1-6

He got up every morning, about 4:30 a.m., made himself a little bit of breakfast, ate it, had some coffee, said his prayers, put on his coveralls and boots, and hopped in the truck. He drove from his home, a modest home that had been in his family for generations, drove along the barbed-wire fence, racing the sunrise, racing the morning flocks of jays and crows, sparrows, and swallows, landing and feeding and chirping and taking off again. He had learned their songs a long, long time ago and the birds in turn had learned that his presence meant them no harm, so they gathered together on the ground and watched as the wheels on his old pickup truck rolled by, leaving little trails of dust in the dry months, and steam in the cold months. It was a little over a mile between his home and the pole barn where his tractor, planter, hay-bailer, and other various pieces of equipment lived. In his younger days he would walk instead of drive, but age, wear and tear, among other realities had lessened his walking. But he still recalled the feeling of being warmed up by the walk, his bones loosening up, his blood giving him time to think about the life he had, the life he had always known.

There were times when he wondered what else was out there, what else might he possibly do. The dirt underneath his fingernails was trace DNA from the legacy his father, grandfather, and great grandfather have handed down to him. There wasn't much else he could think of doing for a living—maybe fishing, maybe woodworking—farming was in his blood. Farming was his blood. He knew his soil and his soil knew him. He had hung in through the lean years and relished the fat years. Still, it wasn't about the money anymore. It was about sustaining life. It was about staying connected. These were his fields and there was always work to be done. Farming. The kind of farmer he was is a rare and dying species these days.

Between his legs on the beat-up bench seat of his truck was a thermos. In that thermos was coffee, black and strong. He twisted the cap off and smiled as the steam and the aroma wafted up. He took a sip and felt the heat glide through his body. The best part of waking up . . . the familiar jingle played in his thoughts. Just a few years before, he would have lingered at breakfast, he would have lingered in his prayers, he would have glanced across the table to see his beloved bride of forty-three years sitting in the chair that was his mother's; he would have smiled as he got up to put his dishes in the sink, and he would have kissed her goodbye saying he would be back at lunch. He would have held on to her hand just a little longer before walking out to his truck. He has grieved and mourned every day for her—made deals with God, made deals with the devil to no avail.

He had adjusted, swallowed the loss, and looked for her beauty in the wings of the feeding birds, the colors of the sunrise, the smell of wood smoke, the way the seasons painted his farm month to month. She wore those colors well, he thought. She wore those colors well.

The kids—his son, his daughter, his princess, and his prince—had grown up and moved away, dodging the duty of the farm, swatting it away with their college degrees and their pursuit of a cleaner way of living: one that offered them well-manicured lawns, commuter traffic, a slew of grocery stores to choose from, and a smattering of 5Ks to run for this charity or that non-profit. They ran. He farmed. They both offer their bodies in various ways to benefit the world around them. But their 5Ks and their kids' sporting events kept them busy and away. He tried not to take it personally. They invited him to come and visit, to come out of exile, but he said the crops needed him, needed him to tend to them, and the fields couldn't be left for too long. Secretly in his heart, the farmer wondered if he managed to get away to see his kids and grandkids, if he would he be able to leave them. In those bleak moments he wondered: Am I working or am I running? Am I working or am I hiding? But he shook the thoughts loose, took another sip of coffee, opened the door, and slid out of the seat. Boots on the ground, tractor in his sights.

Night was the hardest time. He was a grown man, a tough man, a strong man. Night brought with her the loneliness of loss.

He read the magazines that had collected beside his armchair. He ate his dinner, did the dishes. He had given up TV a long time ago saying there wasn't anything worth watching now that all the good shows are off the air. He sat in his chair—the one that has molded to the form of his body—and he read, faster and faster, trying to keep his eyes and mind occupied, trying hard to find some way of outrunning the tears, but they came. They always came. And he wept. Wept for his wife, his kids, even the old mutt that used to keep him company, for friends who had gone on to their great reward, for the shadows of his mother and father that still hung around in the halls and on the walls of his house. No one there to comfort him, to dry his eyes, to hold him. The only thing that brought him any kind of comfort at all was knowing that night would end, the morning would come, and his fields will be waiting for him. The only living memory that tied him to his place were his fields. He laid down his head on the pillow, crying out to God: Help me let it go. Help me let it all go. This place is my graveyard. Tombs. My mother, my father, my grandfather, my grandmother, my wife—my sweet beautiful loving wife, and my children want nothing to do with this place. Help me find peace. Help me find release. Help me let it go. My mouth is filled with bitterness. My old memories have been transformed from ones of joy to ones of torment. I want to love this place, not feel confined by it, but it is all that I know and I am scared to let it go. Help me, God.

And morning comes, just like it does every day. He gets up, eats a bit of breakfast, pulls on his coveralls and boots, and heads out to the fields. Every thought of letting this place go has crawled back into the recesses of his mind. They rarely show up while the sun is rising and gliding across the sky. The light gives him strength, the sun beats back the shadows, and he is at peace again riding in the cabin of his truck. For a moment he looks back at his house through his rearview mirror, remembers bringing his bride home, welcoming his firstborn into the world, pushing his youngest in the tire swing that dangled underneath the oak leaves, peppering the ground with acorns. He remembers the struggles that they faced around the table, and that they always paused for prayer before a meal. He remembers the comfort the teakettle offered at the end of a cold afternoon out in the fields, and how soothing it was to watch his children sleep beneath their blankets, leaving his heart feeling full, even grateful.

This place has lost its light. This place has lost its life. These are hard words to contemplate for the farmer. It's not even dusk yet and the words and thoughts are braving the light to come out of hiding to spend the day with him out in the fields. The farmer remembers and laments and grieves and chokes down the bitter tears. His grandkids will never swing under the canopy of the white oak. His grandkids will never run to the screen door to wait for him to return from the fields. His grandkids will never come and dwell in this place. And he can't bring himself to let it go—even though it is in ruins.

How lonely sits this house that once was full of people. How like a widow I have become. I weep bitterly in the night with tears on my cheeks and there is no comfort. My friends are all but gone, my family all but gone. They are almost like strangers. My kids have taken off for the city to work and here, in my home, I find no resting place. I mourn as I make my way down the road. I see fences that need fixing, barbed wire that needs mending. I make mental notes that slip away. All of it is slipping away. Help me, God. Help me to let it go instead of watching it slip away. Restore me, Lord. I am afraid. I remember this place in its heyday. Now I am shocked when I see it as faded, broken. I have survived. I remember. I long for the days when this place was so full of life.

The farmer takes a long draw from his thermos, shakes the thoughts from his head, pulls his coat closer to his body, and begins a long day out in his fields knowing fully that part of his job now, in the world he lives in, is to tell the story of how this place used to shine like a city on a mountaintop: a house so full of love and life, a place that burned bright with faith. He won't let that go. It is in his remembering that he finds solace and comfort. Amen.

How lonely sits the city
that once was full of people!
How like a widow she has become,
she that was great among the nations!
She that was a princess among the provinces
has become a vassal.

She weeps bitterly in the night,
with tears on her cheeks;
among all her lovers
she has no one to comfort her;
all her friends have dealt treacherously with her,
they have become her enemies.

Judah has gone into exile with suffering
and hard servitude;
she lives now among the nations,
and finds no resting place;

her pursuers have all overtaken her
in the midst of her distress.

The roads to Zion mourn,
for no one comes to the festivals;
all her gates are desolate,
her priests groan;
her young girls grieve,
and her lot is bitter.

Her foes have become the masters,
her enemies prosper,
because the Lord has made her suffer
for the multitude of her transgressions;
her children have gone away,
captives before the foe.

From daughter Zion has departed
all her majesty.
Her princes have become like stags
that find no pasture;
they fled without strength
before the pursuer. (Lamentations 1:1–6)

Antiques Roadshow

Sometimes you just need to watch
a little Antiques Road Show
to remember what it looks like
to find value
not in the items
brought to the experts
but in the stories

about the artist
the art
the family member
who passed the item down.
No matter what the dollar value is on
the vase/painting/gun/furniture/odd jewelry or what
    have you
the story is always priceless.

Some Questions for Your Consideration

1. If you could pick one thing to take to the Antiques Roadshow, what item would you pick?

2. What is the story behind that item?

3. Do you plan to pass it along to someone?

4. How will you share the story with them?

Keep, Goodwill, Trash, Recycle

I'm cleaning out my closets.
No, that is not a metaphor
and no, I am not going back into the closet.
I am literally cleaning out my closets.
How in the heck did I accumulate so much stuff?
I have found some treasures along the way.
Things I had forgotten about.
Things I hold precious and thought I'd lost
but I never lost the memories.
I'm not a big fan of stuff.
In fact, stuff can sometimes cause me to feel oppressed
repressed, closed in and tight chested with cold sweat.
I like memories better. They are light, don't take up

a great deal of room and I can take them wherever I go.
But here I am, sorting through trinkets, pictures, cards, notes, cds
sweaters, dreams I put on hold, financial documents,
prayer shawls, books I meant to read but haven't yet.
Stuff.
Stuff.
Stuff . . .
The sorting begins.
Keep, Goodwill, trash, recycle
Keep, Goodwill, trash, recycle
Keep, Goodwill, trash, recycle
but my memories, I gather them in my arms,
sit down on the floor like a toddler
and marvel at the life I have lived up to this point
and I am overcome with gratitude and thanksgiving.

An Activity for Your Consideration

One of my favorite Lenten disciplines is the Forty Bags in Forty Days with the object being that every day during Lent you get rid of one bag of stuff. I'm not sure what day of the year it is right now in your world, but file that idea away; Lent is coming.

I Love You Sweet Girl

There is a quietness, a peace about her
stretched out on the sofa, lounging in my bed
snuggled in close which, to be honest, is about three
    inches away from my hip
but I'll take it.
I will take it all.

She is my beloved four-pawed companion
and she has taught me so many languages
and so many expressions of love and joy.
She is getting up there in age
She is also becoming a sweet old soul
I'll focus on the latter for now.
Our walks are shorter
Our mornings have more intention in our movement
and actions before I leave for a day of work.
I make sure the last words I say to her are
"I love you, sweet girl."
What I don't say to her but I whisper in my soul are these
    words
"You are going to break my heart one day."
But a heart broken by love and life
is worth the experience of sharing a life with a being who
wags her tail
sniffs the wind
and loves you completely and unconditionally.

*Ella, my sweet girl, left this world on August 1, 2014. She lived
a full and wonderful life, walked many trails, swam in many
streams, camped like a champ, and enjoyed many Town House®
crackers and bags of microwave popcorn, all the while main-
taining her sweet disposition. She let me know that her time
had come and she asked me to offer her the dignity of dying in
peace and leaving the world on her terms. It was the hardest
part of loving her. Even today I weep for her and the loss of her
presence in my life. She taught me so many ways to love and
express love. I give thanks for her amazing ability to teach, and
her patience with me as I struggled to learn her language. She
learned my language, our language, quickly.*

Two Things

Two things.
Bread, wine
song, prayer
breathe in, breathe out
hold on, let go
growing up, growing old
When I was a kid, two things that could entertain me
     for hours:
digging for worms
hammering nails
I could tell by the look of the soil if we were coming up
     on worms
there was something different in the color, the texture,
     the smell
big plump worms, plopped into a can or a plastic
     container or even
one of our nicer cups
Each one would be the perfect worm to catch a catfish
     or a bream
but I never made it to the pond
and when I had made my peace with that understanding,
     I put them all back
to be caught again.
Nails and hammer, wet and rotted wood—one swing and
     the nail went clean through
I felt powerful, I felt mighty, I felt like with that hammer
     I could do anything
except the things that required gentleness, patience,
     restraint—a hammer isn't really good at those things
And when I was finished, I took all the nails out of the
     worn, old wood, restored.

Two things
love and laughter
Joy and peace
asking and receiving
hoping and knowing
Ashes to ashes
Dust to dust

Some Questions for Your Consideration

1. What were some of your pastimes and hobbies as a kid?

2. Do you still practice that hobby now?

3. Who taught you that activity?

4. Did you ever encounter God while playing or doing your hobby?

5. What was that like?

PRAYING

The first time I remember praying was with my Mom and Dad when I was a very young child. Our nighttime ritual of goodnight kisses and prayer was the first time I realized that I could talk with God. Someone my age, my size, with my lack of experience could, anytime I wanted to, talk with God. I felt like I had a super power in knowing this truth and having a super power at a very young age can change your whole life.

Praying, the art of making time and space to be in relationship with God and to offer to God the hopes, wants, needs, petitions, and thanksgivings that resonate in our own hearts, to create spaces to listen to what God might be saying to us is unique to each of us. How I choose to pray may be very different from the way you choose to pray but the God that loves us is a nimble, flexible God that receives our prayers no matter what form they take.

When I left the church in my early twenties, prayer was a lifeline to the hope that I carried that even if I could not be at home within the building, within the worship that took place within that building, that at least I could still be at home in God. Prayer is also what led me out of my wilderness, gave me the courage to try again, and prayer gave me the strength to cross the threshold of All Souls Cathedral in Asheville, NC carrying my wounds with me and seeking to be healed.

At all times and in all places, we are connected to the one that created us, creates us and loves us and that connection comes in the form of prayer.

Slow Me Down, Lord

Slow me down, Lord; slow me down.

Keep me present, Lord; keep me present.

Let tomorrow take care of itself, Lord; let tomorrow be just tomorrow.

Stir within me, Lord; stir within me.

Make my words gentle, Lord; let my words be gentle.

Wash over me, Lord; wash over me.

Open me up, Lord; open my heart even wider.

Search my soul, Lord; search me and know me.

Remove from me the worry, Lord; remove from me the worry.

Create in me a clean heart, Lord, and renew a right spirit within me.

Replenish my spirt, Lord; replenish my spirt.

Continue to call me, Lord; even when I refuse to listen.

Here I am, Lord; here I am.

Make me ready, Lord; make me ready.

Help me to delight, Lord; help me to delight.

Slow me down again, Lord; slow me down again.

O Lord, hear my prayer.

Some Questions for Your Consideration

1. If you could go back in time and ask the Lord to make your words gentle, would you? What or how would you have said something differently?

2. What would you need in order to feel "ready"? What are you preparing for? What is God preparing you for?

3. Have you ever wondered about some of the ways God calls us, prepares us, tries to slow us down and we can only see or hear those moments after the fact? Where and when has God called you? Prepared you? Slowed you down? Did you know it at the time or did you notice it when reflecting on those moments?

Connected

The stillness of the predawn morning still catches me by surprise. A gift of being present to this dark morning, I caught the shadowy dance of two rabbits moving in my yard. It is easy to slip into this day without being aware of the world around us. Standing with bare feet on the sidewalk, I felt the cold matter beneath my feet and I was connected to and not protected from the world around me. Lord, help me to stay connected. Help me to remind myself to stay connected. Help me to be aware of the simple gifts that being connected offer those who have their eyes and hearts open. Help me to enter this day with hope.

Rising As I Am Able

I sit here sometimes, in the quiet, in the great before, in the waiting.
I sit here and listen to the house running, the heartbeat of electric current keeping things in order.
I sit here and breathe in the aroma of life, the shampoo, the dishwasher liquid, and the remnants of dinner still hanging in the air.

I sit here and feel the sun, bright and distant but getting
closer every day, and stretch my arms right into the
rays.
I sit here and pray for people by name, for whole
countries by name, for me by name and, as if it were
choreographed,
The wind chimes sing, ring, stirred by the spirit, by the
Spirit, singing my prayers into the new day.
I sit here sometimes and think, and dream, and ponder,
and wonder, and hope, and weep, and give thanks.
And then I rise as I am able to begin.
Amen.

A Prayer for the Evening

Loving God
Be with me this evening as
I think about the days ahead of me
And
I think about the days behind me.
Help me to let go of those things that are no longer
mine to
Hold on to.
Help me to free my hands and heart to receive
What is coming towards me
What I am moving towards
What is just around the corner,
Over the next hill
Under my feet.
Within this spirit is a sense of hope
A sense of peace

A sense of quiet understanding
I am where I am supposed to be
Today.
Lord, help me to use all of the gifts you have given me
To serve and love those whose names I don't know,
Especially the ones whose names I don't know.
I pray that the words "I am sorry" never taste bitter or
    like sour wine.
I pray that the words "Forgive me" never feel false in
    meaning or intention.
I pray that the word "beloved" will always describe those
    I agree with and those I disagree with.
You have called us to be one, not to agree—but to be one
Help us to see that we are one around the table
No matter what language we speak
Or what school we attend
Or what place we go for work
Or who we come home to at the end of the day
Or how we envision your presence in our lives.
Amen.

Some Questions for Your Consideration

1. Are you holding onto something that is no longer yours to hold on to?

2. What would it take for you to let that go?

3. What is one gift you want to use but currently are not using?

4. What would it take for you to use that gift?

5. What else gets in the way of our ability to see that we are one around the table?

The Song of Hopes and Thanksgivings

In the quiet stillness of the morning, before the children start arriving at school, before the recycling truck comes banging down the road, before the commute to work, and before the grand dance of this day fully waking up, I add my prayers to the song of hopes and thanksgivings—a song I both know well and I am still surprised by. It is a song our souls know by heart, even when we sometimes forget the lyrics.

I will sing to the Lord as long as I live; I will sing praise to my God while I have being. May my meditation be pleasing to him, for I rejoice in the Lord. (Psalm 104:33–34)

Walking with Gratitude

When you walk with gratitude, you will be amazed by the landscape you leave behind.

An Activity for Your Consideration

In your journal, sketch or color or draw what you imagine a landscape of gratitude looks like.

My Heart as a Witness

There are moments, every once in a while, when I am just undone by the world we live in.
I sometimes feel powerless. I sometimes feel powerful. Rarely do I ever feel hopeless. I guess that is what grace is all about. To see the picture, the small and big picture and rather than running in the opposite direction, we are

invited to sit in that discomfort, feel our way through the maze until we can see the glimmer of hope and possibilities. Sometimes I go looking for this kind of discomfort but most of the time I feel as if the discomfort was seeking me. So I will continue to read the headlines and pray for the love of God to be manifest in the world and at this time and then I am going to stay there and offer my heart as a witness to the goodness that is in this world.

Lord, in your mercy . . .

When We Are Still

Easing into this grey and rainy morning, my body and mind have been slow to stir or move. I feel grateful for a day of rest and give thanks that, even though I have been slow to learn, I now know how to rest.

Much of what I preach and how I live and the places I place my hope and prayer are all in the act of doing but in order to do them well, to live them well, one must rest. Be still.

The spirit speaks when we are still. Be still. We hear when we listen and listening asks us to be still. Be still. Be still long enough to hear the whole message, to pray the whole prayer, to sing the whole song, to remember the whole memory. Be still. Rest. Sabbath.

Some Prayers Are Wordless

And when I open my mouth to pray and no words come out, I am neither afraid nor disappointed. Some moments escape words, some prayers are wordless; and sometimes it is better to be a witness in prayer than a wordsmith in action.

● An Activity for Your Consideration

In your journal, just doodle a prayer using no words.

Settling Around Us

Night settles all around us. First the words, then the images, then the hopes, and finally our prayers, all settling around us. I wrap my prayers around me like a blanket or a scarf, place them close to my heart—little words, big words, filled with the emotion that only prayers can contain. I love you. I am worried. I rejoice with you. I hold you close. I lift you up.

I give what I can't carry over to God knowing that God's hands are more experienced and can carry what I cannot. Lord, be with us, in our breath and in our blood. Be with us in the sun setting, the moon rising, and in the sleep that surrounds us. This. This is your work, and we are your hands. Bless every palm that holds the heart of our neighbors, and be with our neighbors who hold our own hearts. Amen.

● An Activity for Your Consideration

Imagine that the space in your journal is God's hands. What is it that you need to give to God knowing that God's hands are more experienced and can carry what you cannot? Draw or write that in your journal.

Morning Prayer

Gracious God, Be the peace that I seek, the love that I
give, the hope that I carry, the light that I walk in, and
the dream of this new day. This is my prayer.

Gracious God, Be the peace that I seek, the love that I
give, the hope that I carry, the light that I walk in, and
the dream of this new day. This is my prayer.

Gracious God, Be the peace that I seek, the love that I
give, the hope that I carry, the light that I walk in, and
the dream of this new day. This is my prayer.

Gracious God, Be the peace that I seek, the love that I
give, the hope that I carry, the light that I walk in, and
the dream of this new day. This is my prayer.

Make these words more than words and give the peace
of Jesus. Amen.

*For surely I know the plans I have for you, says the Lord,
plans for your welfare and not for harm, to give you a future
with hope. Then when you call upon me and come and pray
to me, I will hear you. When you search for me, you will find
me; if you seek me with all your heart. (Jeremiah 29:11–13)*

What If. Why Not.

What if. Why not.
These two phrases, sentences, are invitations to seek,
wonder, discover, discern.
    What if? Why not?
These two little, tiny, two-word questions have gotten me
into so much trouble.

They have also allowed me to dream larger than my own mind and understanding.

If, why, suppose, wonder. . . . Jesus lived in between the concrete and intangible, between the black and white. These statements allow us to explore where, why, how, when, and if. . . . oh if—you are my deepest depth of seeking.

If there is

If I am

If it is

If

I've got no grand illusions that life reveals itself in blatant neon signs.

We have no recourse in our deepest yearnings to be exposed to such clear understandings

Because the journey to this point has been paved by dotted lines, blurry exposes, and holy questions.

Jesus says, "I am in the Father and the Father is in me." But what if that same being is in me as well—

Then what?

What.

What?

God invites us into the blurry and into the grey. God says, I want you to experience me here, now—in the murky and muddy because this is where you came from. This is the mud from which you were created and through which your sight was given. Meet me here. Meet me here in this muck and mire so when you see me clearly, you know that it is me, moving in the world around you, moving in the world through you. Here are our deepest prayers, deepest longings: to not only see God at work in our world, but to also experience God through our relationships with one another. What if, the relationship I have with you is God inspired? Why not see God at work in us?

Why not.

What if? I try hard not to ask how come—because God is able to dwell in the doubt, but work is done in the risk of overcoming doubt and seeing our way into the reality of today.

Today.

Today I give thanks for all the muck and mire that has dwelled in my own life. It is in that darkness that the glory of God has truly been revealed—beyond my expectation and understanding.

Thank you God for being willing to meet me in the mud of my own existence and showing me that even there Love is offered, trust is given, and risks are worth taking. Amen.

A Question for Your Consideration

1. What if. . . . (Come on, you knew it was coming.) Why not. . . .

A Not So New Zealand Prayer for the Afternoon

Lord, it is afternoon. The afternoon is for the gym. Let us workout in the presence of others who are sweating. It is afternoon after a very long day. What has been done has been done; what has not been done has not been done— except those miles and sit-ups and weights. Don't you dare let it be. You better get yourself to the gym and sweat!

The afternoon is far from quiet. Let the noise bring about a sense of peace that you could have just gone home but didn't. . . . So there. Let those who also made that choice enfold you: those who are dear to us and those who grunt too much while lifting making all kinds of noise.

The afternoon heralds the evening, which means a long walk with the puppies. Let us look expectantly to saying, "Stop. Riley. Christ, Riley. Come here. Come here. Come here, come here, come here. Let's go. Stop. Quit eating Lady's leash." In your name we pray. Amen.

Where Today Ends and Tomorrow Begins

We went sailing one night after the darkness settled in for a good stretch of time. We were on an adventure that contained one boat, two hearts, the wide open sea, and the even wider open sky.

We let the sound of the sea settle into our bones, drank in the silence between our voices, and reveled in the conversations our hearts were having with God.

"There is no better place to pray than here on the sea." You said to me.

"I know this church well." I answered back.

We sailed out to the buoy that symbolized the end of the estuary and the beginning of the real ocean. We kept going.

Sometimes you just have to go where you can't hear artificial.

We kept going. You knew the spot you wanted us to reach, and I relaxed into the boat a little bit, feeling grateful that I had decided—at the last minute—to grab a sweatshirt. You started humming the last hymn we sang at Compline, and I felt the peace that eludes me most of the time hunker down with me, covering me as close as my own skin.

"Summer will be ending soon." You said in the same tone that I make announcements in church on Sundays. The content is obvious but somehow it sounds truer when stated in a voice other than my own.

"Yes," I said. "It seems to be going by way too fast these days." That was the truth then and it is the truth today.

I would have given anything to extend that day, that week, that month, that summer just a little longer in order to truly appreciate the sacredness and goodness that came from that holy place. But life calls us forward, all the while explaining that there are other curves and mountains and valleys ahead on our journey. There are pains and hurts and devastations that happened after that night and throughout the twenty-plus years since that I wish that I could have avoided, but who would I be otherwise?

Prepare the way of the Lord.

We slowed down, surrounded by the water and the sky, and I caught a glimpse of your silhouette outlined by the light of the heavens. Your forehead, the bridge of your nose, the tussle of your hair beaten about by the whip of the wind, and the slope of your shoulder to your upper arm steering us to the place you longed to show me.

"What do you pray for when we worship?" you asked.

I took my time in answering because the weight of your question deserved my consideration. After all, you were welcoming me into your church and I wanted to respect the rites and rituals of the way you connect to God.

"You know . . ." I paused. "I spend most of my time in prayer thanking God." I let that response dissipate into the night air before I continued. "And then I ask God to please be patient with me. After that, I kind of let my mind wander." That was the truth back then and it is the truth today. "What about you?" I asked.

A long pause occurred as your words formed in your heart before you gave them voice. After a while you replied, "Most of the time I am just listening."

I took a moment to ponder your response. Then I asked, "Has God ever said anything?"

"Yes. Once."

I was a little surprised but I had to ask, "What? What did God say?"

"God said, 'Meet me at the horizon where today ends and tomorrow begins and you will see that I am there in both—always have been and always will be. I am the Alpha and the Omega.' I come here to meet God, where the sky and ocean meet, and I finish my prayers here."

Silence fell upon us as I marveled at the place where you worship and I let the rhythm of the water below be the drone in my own prayer. It was in the darkness and the peace of the stillness that I experienced God that evening. I have never felt so small or so treasured in my entire life. That was the truth back then and it is the truth today.

I remember you.

I remember the ocean.

And I remember seeing God that night in the tenderness of your heart. Amen.

HEART, SOUL, AND MIND CONVERSATIONS

I am certain that when I am asleep, my heart, soul, and mind have conversations that the rest of me is not privy to. I am also certain that my heart, soul, and mind have very distinct personalities of their own and that these personalities inform how those secret conversations go. I may be a little silly, but I believe each of us has within us a heart, soul, and mind that shade and impact the conversations we have in our private thoughts, the way we prepare for the day ahead, the way we reflect on the day behind us, and the way we connect to God. I can't prove this suspicion, but I can write about my own experience with these three parts of my being which is exactly what I did for one month.

What follows is a series of conversations: a spark, a glimpse into how my mind, soul, and heart talk with one another when the rest of the world isn't paying attention. I wrote a daily thought at the beginning of each day for thirty-one days that I thought might be a place for you to begin to listen to your own heart, mind, and soul conversations. I believe that how we choose to begin the day has a genuine impact on how we experience the rest of our day. Spending a little time listening to our heart, soul, and mind before we begin our day is time well spent.

There are no rules. You can read them all in one sitting or you can read one at a time over the next thirty-one days or you can just skip this part of the book. Be forewarned, however, that I believe in the innocence of these three entities, and that the seed that they are grown from comes from a place of goodness, light, love, and God. These daily meditations are sparks of light, a little funny, perhaps hopeful, and above all, written from my heart, soul, and mind to yours.

DAY ONE

"Quit looking at the calendar," my soul said to my mind. "You can't make it speed up and you can't make it slow down."

"But can I find a pause button?" asked my mind. "There are some moments I would like to linger in just a little longer."

DAY TWO

"What is the best Way to approach Today?" asked my heart.

"With our heart softened, our mind open, and our spirit relaxed," said my soul. "It is easier to absorb what comes your way than to resist."

DAY THREE

"Sometimes the quiet can be rather loud," said my mind. "When I get still, I realize that there is so much going on that I haven't paid attention to."

"That is what prayer is for," replied my soul. "Prayer is big enough to hold the quiet. There are some things our human language cannot express, and for that reason we have smiles, tears, dreams, and hugs."

DAY FOUR

"Sometimes the most frightening thing a person can do is tell the truth," said my soul, "and many times truth-telling is the beginning of an amazing adventure."

DAY FIVE

"I like how this looks on us," said my heart.

"How what looks on us?" asked my mind.

"Gratitude," responded my heart. "Never out of season, no matter what time of year."

DAY SIX

"What are we going to do today?" asked my heart.

"Finish and play," said my soul.

"In that order?" asked my heart.

"Always. . . . Finishing work makes play play and not a distraction," said my soul.

"Yeah. But distractions can be so fun," spoke my heart.

"True. Very, very true."

DAY SEVEN

"Sometimes you have to give and give until you reach the bottom of the bucket," said my heart.

"And then what?" asked my mind.

"And then you give them the bucket," my heart replied.

DAY EIGHT

"Sometimes change hurts. Sometimes letting the world form you and shape you can be painful," said my heart. "And sometimes change can feel like a hug from a friend, a setting down of a heavy burden, a whisper of a prayer into the chorus of morning."

DAY NINE

"Sometimes things don't go according to the plan," my soul spoke. "And sometimes they turn out much better than you could have ever imagined."

DAY TEN

"I feel like something strange is happening inside of me," said my heart.

"Me, too," said my soul.

"I feel strange as well," said my mind.

"I think we might be in bloom," said my heart.

DAY ELEVEN

"Why on Earth are you up?" my soul asked my mind.

"I was dreaming of the future and I got so excited I couldn't sleep," my mind replied.

"Even in the future you will need to rest, dear mind. Go back to bed."

DAY TWELVE

"I woke hungry and thirsty today," said my heart.

"Ahhhh," said my mind. "Then it worked."

"What do you mean?" asked my heart.

"You enjoyed yesterday so much you woke up hungry for more life," replied my mind.

"Yep. That sounds about right," said my heart.

DAY THIRTEEN

"Sometimes you just have to be bold and brave and ask for what you want," said my soul.

"How do you know what you want?" asked my heart.

"You start the day—each day—with the same idea swimming around in your mind, trying not to open your mouth for fear it might spill out; then that want doesn't belong to you anymore but to the whole world," replied my soul.

"But if you can't open your mouth because you don't want the world to know your want, then how are you fed?" asked my heart.

"Exactly!" answered my soul.

DAY FOURTEEN

"Oh. I am so full. I couldn't possibly take in another thing," said my heart.

"Then try giving some of yourself away and see if that helps," my soul spoke. "Nope. That didn't work. I feel even fuller now," replied my heart.

"Funny how that happens."

DAY FIFTEEN

Then my soul spoke and said, "Shhh. Sometimes your mind talks too much. Ask your heart. She has a great deal to say."

DAY SIXTEEN

"What are you doing?" asked my mind.

"I'm learning the story and the song of my sisters, aunts, mothers, and grandmothers," replied my heart.

"Why?" my mind questioned.

"So I can teach it to my nieces, daughters, and granddaughters," my heart answered.

"Is it long?" inquired my mind.

"It is as long as it needs to be."

DAY SEVENTEEN

"Every once in a while I look up and take a look around me," said my heart. "I see the city, the people. I hear the rhythm and the pulse, and I realize I am right where I need to be."

"But don't you miss where we used to be?" asked my mind.

"Every day," said my heart.

"I miss that place, but I don't want to miss being here by lamenting not being there. We have to love where we are, right where we are, otherwise we miss the whole point."

"Agreed," said my soul and mind.

DAY EIGHTEEN

"Eeehhhhhkkkkk," said my mind. "I have morning breath."

"Not possible. You must have dream breath," said my soul.

"Why do you say that?" my mind asked.

"You haven't been awake long enough to taste the morning, but you have been chewing on your dreams all night. Dream breath," said my soul.

"So it is. I have a wicked case of dream breath," said my mind."

"Me, too," said my soul.

DAY NINETEEN

"Sometimes I just don't know what else to say," said my heart. "How many times can a heart say thank you?"

"Every day, for the whole of your life," spoke my soul.

DAY TWENTY

"Did you feel that?" asked my heart. "That was me laying down a burden."

"Ahhhh," said my soul. "I feel better."

"What are you going to do now?" chimed my mind.

"I don't know, but I have two free hands and a lighter soul to do it with."

DAY TWENTY-ONE

"All my words have holes in them," spoke my soul. "They aren't able to hold all the love I want to share."

"There are some things you can't undo with words, and there are some things words can't touch," said my heart. "In those moments you offer love, you offer prayers and you offer presence—even if you are a million miles away."

DAY TWENTY-TWO

"I want to give something that will last forever," my heart spoke.

"Nothing lasts forever," chimed my mind.

"Heart, you can't give a memory, but you can help create one. Memories do last forever," whispered my soul.

DAY TWENTY-THREE

"Do you ever just really want something?" my soul asked. "I mean like want. Want with all of your . . . soul? You just think about it all the time—that kind of want?"

"Like how I wanted to sleep in this morning," my mind remarked.

"No, bigger, deeper, want."

"Yeah," my heart spoke. "I know that kind of want. I pray that if I ever get what I want that I will recognize the gift of that moment and not forsake it by immediately wanting something else."

"Me, too," said my soul.

"Me three," said my mind.

DAY TWENTY-FOUR

"Don't forget," said my heart.

"Don't forget what?" asked my mind.

"Don't forget to stop from time to time and take it all in. Otherwise you might just miss how amazing this life is."

DAY TWENTY-FIVE

"Looking back on the whole experience up to this point, is one of my favorite ways to spend time in the morning," said my heart.

"It is also one of my favorite ways to pray," replied my soul.

DAY TWENTY-SIX

"You know what I am grateful for?" asked my heart.

"What?" replied my mind.

"That you don't need boxes to take hope, love, and faith with you into the next part of the journey. That could get expensive and heavy quickly," answered my heart.

DAY TWENTY-SEVEN

"Looks like someone spilled crumbs all over our calendar," my heart said.

"Nope. That's just the schedule for Holy Week," my mind replied.

Lord have mercy. . . .

DAY TWENTY-EIGHT

"Do you hear that?" my heart whispered. "That is the sound of possibility."

"It just sounds like rain to me," my mind responded.

"Falling at your feet . . . ," my heart giggled.

DAY TWENTY-NINE

"Are you ready?" asked my soul.

"I think so," said my mind.

"Me, too," said my heart.

"Okay, then," replied my soul. "On the count of three. One. . . . Two. . . . Three," and the snooze button was pushed. Sometimes making sure to savor the morning is a collective initiative between my heart, soul, and mind.

DAY THIRTY

"How come breakfast doesn't have a dessert menu?" asked my mind.

"You have the whole day ahead of you—that is dessert enough," said my soul.

I'm diving deep into this dessert and taking a few laps. Blessed Sabbath rest.

DAY THIRTY-ONE

"How did this happen?" my soul asked.

"How did what happen?" replied my mind.

"How is it that we are at the end of the heart, mind, and soul conversation already?" continued my soul.

"I'm not sure there is an explanation, but I am certainly glad that I reached this day with you," said my heart.

"And the truth is," my mind continued, "this conversation is really just beginning."

What is the conversation like this morning or afternoon or evening between your heart, mind, and soul? In your journal, doodle or write what they are saying.

RELEASING

Releasing could be, quite possibly, the hardest spiritual practice or discipline—at least that is my opinion with forty-four years of being a bit of a control freak to back that claim up. Releasing, the act of letting go, is a decision that once made cannot be unmade, and that can be extremely frightening. The weight of carrying around so much in our hearts can be equally frightening and exhausting.

I will admit freely and openly that there are items rolling around in my heart that should have been released ages ago. I am just not ready, not today, but I am hopeful that one day I will have the courage to release what is no longer mine to carry and give it all over to God. I trust that God is big enough and gentle enough to receive what I need to release—I know this in my bones, actually, but the trappings of holding onto these little tiny hurts and expectations can be hard to see around.

Sometimes I imagine my hands filled with marbles, big ones and little ones, all different colors and patterns filling my hands. Although they are beautiful to see, the marbles make life pretty difficult. I can't button my shirt, or make breakfast, or drive my car well—in fact, I can't do anything well because my hands are full. Each marble represents something I should release, something I should let go and give to God, and until I do make that commitment my hands will remain full.

I have found that confession in the daily office or in the Eucharist is a perfect time to start handing stuff over to God, releasing the burden and the weight of carrying so much in our hands and hearts. Saying the words is one thing, but praying the words of confession is very different. When I was first coming back to the church, I prayed the prayer of confession every day for months, not because I was an abnormally sinful person, but because the words I was praying reminded me that I relied on God and confession is a way of saying, "Here, God. Take this away from me. I am not strong enough to let it go without you. Here, help me release what is no longer mine to carry."

If you are struggling with a deep desire to release and make room in your heart and in your hands, find a prayer of confession that resonates within your soul. The Book of Common Prayer's Confession of Sins works for me.

When our hands and heart are free, freed and liberated, then we can receive fully the mercy and grace of our God.

Answers

I don't have all the answers. My heart finally admitted a long-understood truth while in my prayer time this morning. I don't know if I ever thought—honestly thought—I would acquire all the answers, but the chase has been fun, daunting, humiliating, exhausting, and devastating—and that was just today. But here is a truth that has manifested itself at key points along this beautiful journey. No one has all the answers. Ever. Amen. Not even Google or Wikipedia or the Magic 8 Ball'. That being said, I feel the more time I spend living in my community, responding to my community, giving and receiving in my community, the more I learn, the more

I want to know, and the more hands and hearts I count as beloved companions in the day-to-day footfalls of this path I am walking.

I have insights to share and I have insights to acquire. That's about it. When we boil it all down, what we bring to the table is a mixture of what we have and what we want. Around the table we are each fed; at least that is the hope and the dream.

I have an ache inside that comes from witnessing the world fall apart—one war, one bullet, one loss at a time—and I can't help but wonder how we are to be the light in this darkness? Sweet, sweet Jesus, how are we to be the light in this darkness?

How can my little light beam bright enough to shine in the night in Israel, Palestine, Ukraine, Liberia, St. Louis, my own adopted hometown of Wilmington, and every other place that is in peril and pain on this late summer evening? How?

I have to believe that what we have in our hearts, that deep desire and need and want to be good to one another, is still at the very core of who we are and who we have been created to be. To be. A wonderful sentiment to think we are constantly changing and moving and growing and learning, not stagnant or ready to settle, but ready and willing to bring our truer, fuller selves to that table where we receive and give and don't worry if someone is getting more than we are. Instead our truer, fuller selves bring and give all that they have and receive what they need and no one leaves with less than they brought.

Oh God. You search us and you know us. When we can't pray words in a language of our own, you intercede with sighs too deep for words. Lord, we need your sighs. Lord, I need your sighs. I can do without answers or reasons behind the violence and death and pain. I know these are not derived from your grace or love. But how many more must perish until we wake up and hear your call? Until we remember your voice in our hearts and in our minds? Until we feel the desire to seek the peace that passes all understanding? How long, oh Lord? How long?

A Note About the Previous Meditation

At 12:01pm on August 9, 2014, Michael Brown was shot by a police officer in Ferguson, Missouri. He was unarmed. Allegedly he was involved in a robbery at a convenience store. He was only eighteen years old and his name joined a long list of other African-American young men shot, while unarmed, while walking, while standing, or while just being and existing. I wrote this as the protests began in Ferguson and I watched the way my brothers and sisters were met in the streets by a police force so afraid to listen that they clothed themselves with armor, teargas, rubber bullets, and shields.

We, neighbor to neighbor, missed an opportunity to listen, to respond, and to seek first to understand than to be understood. We have had several opportunities to come to the table and orchestrate real and effective changes, but, unfortunately, rather than have that conversation we have pointed fingers, laid blame, cried out that all lives matter. We are missing the point. We cannot begin to claim that "all lives matter" when we get offended by "black lives matter."

Dear Jesus, help us to hear you in the cries of our sisters and brothers and give us the strength to do what is right instead of what is convenient.

Be Not Afraid

Be not afraid.
Be not afraid.
I mean, it is okay if you feel afraid
But I'm telling you, don't waste any time
Trying to figure out why you are afraid
Be not afraid.
Be not afraid.
Since you are sitting there thinking about
How this might play out or might not play out,
I'm just saying, don't be afraid.
Yes, there is mystery
And there is unease
And dis-ease
But don't be afraid.
I've got you.
I've always had you
And this too shall pass.
Be not afraid.
Love,
God.

A Little Note About the Previous Poem

I was diagnosed in May 2009 with rheumatoid arthritis. The two months leading up to that diagnosis were probably the two scariest months of my entire life. The mystery, the pain, the God-awful pain, and the loss of control. Both knees, both feet, both wrists, both elbows, and my back were affected.

I. Was. Scared.

I still get scared from time to time. The difference between today and 2009 is that I know the name of what is causing my fear and I know who I need to call and then I know what protocol to follow. I also know that the fear in me is something I need to turn over to God because when I am in a state of having a flare-up, there isn't much I can hold on to. What I have learned over the past couple of years is my fear is not about pain. It is about losing my independence. But in faith and following our spiritual journey, we are to surrender, daily, all of who we are to God. Knowing that little bit helps take away some of the fear. Having experienced God standing strong with me in my weakness has helped alleviate the rest of my fear in my disease and in my life.

Water

Water.

It is what first holds us. Before we ever know the touch of human hands, the feeling of air on our skin, the color of light, we know water.

Water.

I came out to God sitting on a dock in the middle of the night surrounded by water. I sought the very essence of my beginning, the element I first knew in order to find the strength to say the words I had carried for so long in my blood, in my mouth, in my soul. I released those words into the element I knew to be strong enough to hold my greatest fear; a part of me because in the beginning it held all of me.

I'm gay. I said it over and over and over to the rhythm of the water lapping at the underside of the dock, and when I couldn't say it any more, I cried tears. Water and salt blended in the heat of my body, the heat of the summer evening, the heat of my fear and sadness, and just like that—released. Undone. All gone. Washed away.

Water.

Nothing stills me quite like water. Ocean, lake, river, rain. Nothing reminds me of how small I am and how big this world is, how big God is, quite like water. I am made of water and I am connected to the water. To the water in others. We, without knowing each other, share the bond of water. When the storms are raging within—torrents of fear, uncertainty, doubt, pain—I am quieted by the embrace of another, by a place to lay my head, by a touch that speaks quietly to my sea and says, "Be still and know . . . be still and know . . . be still and know that I am God and you are loved. Be still."

Water.

On the eve of the day when a decision would be made that would affect and change my life forever, sleep eluded me, taunted me, hid from me, and I chased its shadow down to the lake. This night in May, underneath Centaurus, Virgo, and Crux I, with my back against the smooth wood, arms wide open, I imagined a million what-ifs as the rolling water underneath rocked, rocked, rocked me to stillness. And then it was quiet. The what-ifs drifted away on the current of the wind and I dipped my hand into the chill of the water to remind myself of my baptism, of my birth, of my connection to God and this earth, my connection to you and what that is worth.

Water.

The last sunny day in July, I drove along a familiar road to a place I had been to a million times before. I ate of the fruit in the valley, and drove up the hills and around the rocks until I saw my destination. I planted myself beside the falls to read and dream, weep and sing, and say my goodbyes to the mountain. As hot as it was, the water was cold. I cupped some in my hands and poured it over my head. Three times. Three times. Three times. And each time it carried away tears. My water. Your water. The water of the mountain. I was now a part of the cycle that, over time, cuts away rock, that moves mountains, that gives life to the foliage that will flow into new life. I may not be there, but I will always be there.

Water.

Some Questions for Your Consideration

1. What in this world reminds you of how small you are?
2. What in this world reminds you of how we are connected one to another?
3. Where have some of the heartfelt conversations between your heart and the heart of our God taken place?
4. Where or what do you draw stillness from?
5. How do you offer stillness to others?

New Year's Revolution

She "didn't mean anything by it"—at least that is what she said when she noticed the implied handprint her remark left on the soul she was speaking to.

"Honestly," she continued while looking down at a loose thread unraveling in her sweater.

The last time she held her breath this long was when she was waiting for God to meet her halfway. Silly child. God never meets us halfway. God always meets us right where we are, even when that makes us uncomfortable.

The pause and silence was so heavy, so all consuming. They were reduced to subtle gestures, breathing, taking space while one waited for the other to continue.

There is a certain delicious anticipation that occurs in the waiting, when you know you can't say anything, all you can do is listen. She said the only thing she could think of. The tried and true, overused, almost meaningless, "I'm sorry." She might as well have said, "Blue ketchup," because that is what it felt like to the one hearing her speak. Just two words, no heart attached, wasting breath and time.

The other leaned in close, close enough to fog the glasses she was wearing. "I know you are afraid," the voice spoke softly. "I know you are afraid and scared and worried, and that your flippant remark that you didn't mean anything by is you trying real hard to railroad me off of the path. I get it. I'm scared too. But listen. I've been in your shoes. I've seen your point of view, and I woke up this morning knowing that this day, this day was too important not to honor with offering all of who I am, all of who God has created me to be to this day and the days to come."

"Yeah, but—" she started, but the other wouldn't let her finish.

"No. You've had your chance to talk, now is your turn to listen. I'm not done." Inhale. "I love you. I have loved you as long as I can remember, but I know that in order for me to take care of me, I have to change, and I know you don't like that. You never have. And I'm not talking about changing my hairstyle, or my wardrobe, or even the place I call home. I mean changing how I talk to myself, how I love myself, how I celebrate who I am, how I start each day, and how I end each night. I have to do this. I really don't have another option anymore. If I don't start loving and respecting who I am, who God has created me to be, how in the hell can I expect the world around me to love me and respect me? I've got gifts, God-given gifts, that need to be unearthed and brought into the light. I have dreams I want to explore. I have a wild and unruly hope that is just jumping at the chance to dance and fly, and I cannot hold onto that hope if I am holding onto you." Exhale.

She stared at her reflection in the bathroom mirror just a little longer before concluding her conversation with a kiss for good luck and a, "Happy New Year!"

And, with that, she left last year behind her.

Do not remember the former things, or consider the things of old. I am about to do a new thing; now it springs forth, do you not perceive it? I will make a way in the wilderness and rivers in the desert. (Isaiah 43:18–19)

Bring Me Your Rawest Self

Bring me your rawest self. Bring me the bits of you that haven't seen light in years. Bring me the wounds that have happened to you and the ones you have caused to the people closest to you. Bring me those wounds you dare not even remember.

Bring me the items in your house and home and life that are beacons of pride. Beacons of pride that cast great light and even longer shadows.

Bring me the words you have spoken that tasted of venom. Bring me the words you have absorbed spoken to you, spoken at you that left marks on your skin and scars on your heart.

Bring me the daydreams you have had that encapsulate a life you would rather live. Who is in that daydream? Who are you in that daydream?

Bring me the stories of your ancestors; bring me the legacy of your name: the name you are called, the name I have called you by.

Bring me the thousands of "I'm sorrys" you have said and meant. Bring the sorrys you said but didn't mean. Bring the sorrys you meant to say but forgot.

Bring me the hope that you carry into each new day. Bring me the love that is alive in your blood and in your bones, the one that fuels you, that frees you; the one you sometimes wonder when you first felt it pulsate in your veins.

Bring me the visions you have of your tomorrows: the laughter you share, the laughter you long for, the laughter that comes from a place that knows and understands true freedom.

Bring me the one thing you plan to carry with you from this life to the next. Did you buy it? Did you make it? Was it given to you?

Bring all this to me, put it down on the floor. I will mix it with clay, fold everything into the clay and create a wondrous work of art. A beautifully flawed and blemished masterpiece, a vessel that I love, a vessel that contains love, a vessel made with love that carries my fingerprints on its interior and exterior. A vessel I call beloved.

Bring me your rawest self. It is the rawness of you that I take into my hands and work, rework, destroy, create, love, and liberate until it is rendered whole, rendered able; rendered and revealed. Bring me your rawest self and I will make you new.

Yet, O Lord, you are our Father; we are the clay, and you are our potter; we are all the work of your hand. (Isaiah 64:8)

○ Some Questions for Your Consideration

1. What is a part of your rawest self?
2. How does that rawness form and shape you?
3. How does God work through that raw part of you?
4. Is there anything about that rawness that you would change?

What I Want You to Know

What I want—more than anything—is to tell you that you are beautiful. You are a masterpiece created by hands that only know how to create beauty. You are a precious gift to this world and one that is, by your sheer being, worthy of a love that goes beyond words. What I want to tell you more than anything is that you are beloved, even in your dark and messy moments; you are beloved beyond the grasp of words. What I want to tell you more than anything is that you are a gift, a blessing, and this world wouldn't be the same without you. What I want you to know is you matter. Your being has worth and your presence is important. Just in case you were wondering!

○ An Activity for Your Consideration

1. Tell someone today how much you love them and how much you appreciate them. Sometimes the only face of Christ a person may see is yours.

And the Weight Shifted

For years I have lived with a state of mind
That values getting it right
Over everything else.
It is how I'm wired—at least
That is what the personality inventories
Have said.
For years my prayer has always been
Am I doing this right?
Or
I hope I am doing this right.
Focusing on the process, on the outcome
But very little of my own spirit infused
Into the meticulousness of each foot step
Get it right
Or don't do it at all.
I missed out on so much.
But something happened along the way
An epiphany of sorts
On a pinnacle—not on the temple
But on a hike—the highest peak
I could find nearby
I looked out over the peaks and valleys below
Sunshine, shadows of clouds, little villages, and roads
And I realized my prayer had been all wrong
For a long, long time.
And I heard the voice of wisdom whisper in the wind
Blowing gently at the top of that trail
"Try this prayer instead:
I am doing the best that I can."
And the weight of the world shifted.

Whatever your task, put yourselves into it, as done for the Lord and not for your masters, since you know that from the Lord you will receive the inheritance as your reward; you serve the Lord Christ. (Colossians 3:23–24)

Some Questions for Your Consideration

1. What, if anything, in your process might be getting in your way of offering more of you?
2. If you have an answer to question 1, why do you think this item is a part of your process?
3. What might you do differently?
4. If Wisdom was to show up one day and offer you some feedback, what do you think she would say?

'Twas the day before Palm Sunday

'Twas the day before Palm Sunday
And all through the church
Men and women were gathered
The Passion play they rehearsed
And the Altar Guild were polishing
The silver and brass with care
They knew that Holy Week
Soon would be here.
The palms they were stripped
Prepared for the next day
When we would hold them up high
and in the air they would sway
Around the church in each of the beds
Mulch was being unloaded, shoveled and spread.
The choir has practiced the anthems so sweet
The priests are preparing to wash everyone's feet

The coals have been purchased to burn and to smolder
To be placed in the thurible—a fancy word for incense
    holder
A parade, a supper up in the upper room
a betrayal, a trial and a crucifixion at noon.
But the story doesn't end, oh no, it has just begun
A blessed Holy Week my friends, to each and every one.

A special thank you to every single person who helps the church, the priests, the organists, the music directors get ready for the busiest week of the year: Holy Week. Every single person who polishes the silver and the brass, who assists in getting the flowerbeds ready, who participates in any of the services, who brings snacks by the office, who prays for the leadership of their church during Holy Week, the flower guild, the Altar Guild, the choir, the acolytes, and those who come to the services— even though you are tired. The journey from Palm Sunday to Easter Sunday is a beautiful, messy, heartfelt, tiring, trying, amazing journey and your presence is appreciated.

We Are All That Woman at the Well

It was early. She stirred from her bed, breathed in deeply the first breath of the new morning. This was her favorite breath. It was the only one she would take today that wasn't tainted with her internal voice chastising her. The voice mimicked the voices of her neighbors, her former friends, and her relatives. Savoring this moment of peace, she held her breath—a little longer, longer still—until her lungs were screaming to just let go. Just let go, already. You can't put this off any longer. The day is here, and you have work to do.

She was the kind of woman mothers pointed out to their sons and said, "Do not marry a woman like that."

She was the kind of woman mothers pointed out to their daughters and said, "Do not be like her."

She was the kind of woman pitying has become unfashionable.

The casseroles stopped coming after Husband Number Four died—or did he divorce her, or did he just quit? It was hard to keep track with a history as varied and checkered as hers.

She had a lover now, out of necessity. Love is too costly an adventure, and really, she gave up on love after Husband Number One passed away.

She went to the kitchen fire to make some broth for the long day ahead. Fuel for her body.

What she wouldn't give to be able to smile across the table at the man whose fragrance delighted her, whose smile was brighter than the sun, whose look of love could undo any chain around her heart, untie any knot within her stomach, loosen any grief she carried.

But he was already gone. And the man whom she slept beside the night before was gone too. Off to work. Even though her internal voice was loud and obnoxious, it didn't take up any room at the table.

"You really didn't need that last glass of wine before bed."

"The dinner you made was horrible. Horrible."

"If only you would have loved him more, maybe then he wouldn't have died."

"Your children barely speak to you anymore. They couldn't wait to get out of the house."

Every word stabbed, made a jagged cut like a knife on skin that seemed so thick, so calloused, but the truth was she is tender, and straining to keep it all together. Even if it felt like a lie.

Early morning slipped into late morning; it happened every day. It was time to do the laundry and start thinking about dinner. Although it was quiet in her house, it was not quiet in her head, in her heart. No amount of distraction was ever enough. The voice kept talking and talking, shouting and yelling and throwing tiny emotional grenades that did so much damage. She began to believe the words a few years ago. You could tell by the way she walked, carried herself, and moved in the world around her. She tried hard to take up as little space as she could, and even harder not to draw attention to herself.

She grabbed the stone water jar—the one that was dry as a bone—and began the walk to the well. Jacob's well. Jacob met Rachel at a well and he fell for her so hard that he worked fourteen years for her hand in marriage. Fourteen years.

"No one would ever work that hard for me, for my love, out of love." Her internal voice agreed and she felt another sliver of her spirit die. Unloved. Unwelcomed. Unknown.

She approached the well and saw a man there. He was alone.

He spoke, "Give me a drink."

She knew the rules, the customs, the norms. She had been reminded of them for years, ever since she became the talk of the town.

He was a Jew. She was a Samaritan. Jews did not share things with Samaritans. The only way this man would get a drink was to drink from her stone jar, which went against the rules and norms and expectations.

The man spoke to her. Right at her. Not about her, not around her, but he saw her. And he spoke: "If you knew God and knew who I was, you would ask me and I would give you living water." It really didn't make sense because he had no bucket, no way of getting any water out of the well where he was sitting. Yet, even though what he said seemed odd, he was talking to her.

"This is Jacob's well. He gave it to us. Our flocks and families have been watered by this well for generations." Maybe the heat had gotten to this man. He needed some water to cool his head and restore his senses.

"You come to this well because you are thirsty. Every day people return to this well because the water they drew yesterday was not enough, and it will never be enough. The living water—the water that is mine to give and share—will become a living spring gushing up to eternal life."

"Oh, if only. If only I could reclaim part of my day and not have to fetch water every day. I want this water, sir. Please, sir. Let me have some of this living water. I am so thirsty."

"Go. Get your husband."

Shame crossed her face. She met someone along the way who didn't know her and she felt safe in that unknowing. Safe and protected from judgment and chiding. All of that was about to change.

"I . . . I have no husband."

The stranger at the well said, "I know. You have had five husbands and the one you are with now is not your husband."

She readied herself for the torrent of words and judgment to pour out from the stranger. Her internal voice giggled in anticipation. But that torrent never came. The stranger welcomed her instead.

"How? How did you know?" she asked. "You must be a prophet. Tell me what I must do, how to worship, where to worship. For years my ancestors have worshipped here, but you say we must worship in Jerusalem. A woman like me isn't fit for

Jerusalem." She was saying what her internal voice was saying. She was saying what her neighbors were saying. She was saying what everyone in her community would have said: she wasn't fit enough, clean enough, good enough, loved enough to worship in Jerusalem, on the mountain. She wasn't enough.

He said, "Here, there, in-between—all places; Jew, Samaritan—it is in truth and spirit that we worship God. The Father wants those who seek him in spirit and in truth."

She had been honest. She had been truthful. She had been open with this stranger. She had given up denying her past a long time ago. Her honesty had not made this man turn from her. He had not chastised her. He continued to have a conversation with her. She was bold enough in her faith, her baby step faith, to say, "I know the Messiah is coming."

Jesus said, "I am he." And the internal voice, the company she had kept for so many years, was silenced.

She went off to tell her neighbors about this man. She sought out people that she normally hid from. She raised her voice to tell her story, even though she normally ran from anyone trying to tell her the parts they already knew. She risked their stares and their jibes, and she was liberated through the acknowledgment of her sins and hearing the Messiah say, "You. The Father wants you to worship in spirit and in truth." In their brief exchange, she felt known.

And the funniest thing happened.

Her neighbors listened. Her neighbors listened to the point that they started to believe. The grace of God was so abundant that even an outcast Samaritan woman was emboldened, strengthened, liberated, freed, welcomed, known, and loved to the point that her neighbors no longer held onto her past because her present and her presence were a powerful testimony to who this Jesus was.

"If he could do this for her, what could he do for me?" they wondered.

Many Samaritans believed because of this woman's testimony.

She was, in a sense, born again. The people almost didn't recognize her because of the powerful change that had taken place in her life.

Yes, she had five husbands, but that wasn't all that the people knew about her anymore. If she hadn't shared her story, her experience with Jesus, then the community would have missed out on knowing this Samaritan woman better. They would have missed out on believing in Jesus as the Messiah.

It is powerful to think that one person's story could have such a powerful impact on her community. She went from being unloved, unwelcomed, and unknown to loved, welcomed, and known.

I have been that woman at the well. I have my not so shiny bits in my own story, and the weight of those parts became increasingly heavy and cumbersome. Confessing these things and truly feeling forgiven moved the stone away from the well, brought me closer to God, freed me to worship in spirit and in truth. Fantastic.

But if the story stops there, then I miss an opportunity to share that story with others. And if I miss the opportunity to share with others, I might also be missing an opportunity to use the story I have—the life I have—to show that even a soul like me can have my thirst quenched and be transformed.

My friends, you have a story too. Maybe you haven't had five husbands. Maybe a stranger has never showed up out of the blue and changed your life. Maybe the pain and sorrow you bear has never been public knowledge. Maybe, but when Christ shows up and offers you love, kindness, compassion, grace, and mercy through the presence of another, then your story changes. When we share our stories with others, not only do we help them on their journeys, but we might be asked to walk with them. The truth is, when we share, we find our thirst and our internal voices eliminated, again and again and again.

Amen.

A Samaritan woman came to draw water, and Jesus said to her, "Give me a drink." (His disciples had gone to the city to buy food.) The Samaritan woman said to him, "How is it that you, a Jew, ask a drink of me, a woman of Samaria?" (Jews do not share things in common with Samaritans.) Jesus answered her, "If you knew the gift of God, and who it is that is saying to you, 'Give me a drink,' you would have asked him, and he would have given you living water." The woman said to him, "Sir, you have no bucket, and the well is deep. Where do you get that living water? Are you greater than our ancestor Jacob, who gave us the well, and with his sons and his flocks drank from it?" Jesus said to her, "Everyone who drinks of this water will be thirsty again, but those who drink of the water that I will give them will never be thirsty. The water that I will give will become in them a spring of water gushing up to eternal life." The woman said to him, "Sir, give me this water, so that I may never be thirsty or have to keep coming here to draw water." (John 4:7–15)

At Rest, At Peace

I will admit it.
A few days ago when I heard the news of Fred Phelps
taking his final curtain call
his final blog writing
his final moments here on Earth,
I was intrigued.
We all will die.
No one gets out of here alive.
But I can't help but wonder
is he at peace now?
Is he wondering how he got it wrong?
Is he wishing he had spent his latter days
preaching the peace that passes all understanding
rather than hate, violence, brimstone, and
other choice words?
I never met him.
I encountered the protests several times
but when you hang out at all the right places and
with all the right people, you are bound to
have to deal with a little hate speech and a protest or two.
So now, I pray that in the great hereafter
Fred has put his protest signs down,
has sat at the banquet prepared for him and for each of us,
is supping in the company of MLK, Harvey Milk, Amy
    Winehouse, and a host
of heavenly bodies
and that tightness in his chest—fear wrapped around hate
    wrapped around grief, wrapped around doubt
is at rest, is at peace, is held and loved and melted away.
I don't like him.

I don't like him one little bit.
But Jesus asked us to pray for and love our enemies—
   even evil, vile, misguided enemies.
So here it goes:
May Fred's soul and the souls of all the departed rest in
   peace and rise in glory.
Amen.

⬤ An Activity for Your Consideration

We all have that "one" person that we have allowed under our skin, given them a blueprint to our buttons and has learned the special dance of annoyance on our last nerve. Take two minutes and think about that person. Take another two minutes and pray for that person by name. Take another two minutes and try, with all of your being, to love that person. Now repeat this every day, at least once a day, for a month and see if that changes how you feel about them.

A Box Full of Jesus

I have a talking Jesus doll.
He is buff and muscular.
He looks like he did CrossFit
instead of taking the long walk
with a cross.
If you push the right spot on his back
he will tell you, in perfect English, five
stories from the Bible.
He is still in the box that he came in
when my younger brother bought him
and gave him to me as a surprise
present after preaching my first sermon back in 2008.

Why is he still in the box?
I thought he was still in the box as a way to preserve him,
to keep him clean and neat.
That was, until I took a real long and honest look at him
    today
protected by the plastic.
There is an additional blurb under his name. It reads
    JESUS with
God's son in smaller letters under his name.
I realized I kept him in the box because that is how
this kind of Jesus should be kept—a false understanding
of Jesus should be boxed away, for it is in the box we place
    him
that he is allowed to move, and live and have his being.
    This is a
very narrow box, the stories he tells from his box,
    although familiar, are
not the whole story—and in this box he will never know
    death
he will never know resurrection
and neither will anyone who listens to this Jesus.
But the Jesus I met on the street on Monday night
walking to my car—that Jesus
asked me for money—of which I had none to give.
The Jesus I met on Tuesday while leaving the grocery
    store
was hungry, and I gave him an orange.
The Jesus I met last night was a child crying on the front
    stoop
of her house who, when she saw me, smiled and said,
    "HI"

The real-life Jesus doesn't live in a box nor does he quote
    from only
five stories, but from all of our stories, from all of our
    lives
and he looks at each of us, sees us, even the parts we hide
    from,
even from the five dollar bill that was in my pocket on
    Monday night that I didn't share with the Jesus who
    asked for money.
Knowing all of this, still this Jesus says, "Come along with
    me, kid. I can use you."
Box not included.

*When he was sitting on the Mount of Olives, the disciples
came to him privately, saying, "Tell us, when will this be, and
what will be the sign of your coming and of the end of the
age?" Jesus answered them, 'Beware that no one leads you
astray. For many will come in my name, saying, 'I am the
Messiah!' and they will lead many astray." (Matthew 24:3–5)*

*"For I was hungry and you gave me food, I was thirsty and
you gave me something to drink, I was a stranger and you
welcomed me, I was naked and you gave me clothing, I was
sick and you took care of me, I was in prison and you visited
me." Then the righteous will answer him, "Lord, when was it
that we saw you hungry and gave you food, or thirsty and
gave you something to drink? And when was it that we saw
you a stranger and welcomed you, or naked and gave you
clothing? And when was it that we saw you sick or in prison
and visited you?" And the king will answer them, "Truly I
tell you, just as you did it to one of the least of these who are
members of my family, you did it to me." (Matthew 25:35–40)*

What Makes You Happy?

She asked, "What makes you happy?"

We were on the porch of a winery near the Delaware/Pennsylvania border enjoying a glass of a red reserved special blend with hints of leather and plum. The taste of Thanksgiving was slowly slipping off my tongue giving way and making room for the season of Advent where we are drawn into a posture of watching and waiting, hoping and preparing and above all, praying. These Advent actions have been a part of my daily routine but most immediately as I begin to seek and listen for my next call as a priest.

I have already begun to grieve.

I have already begun to grieve some of the loss this journey costs.

I have already begun to grieve with thoughts of, "This time next year . . ."

But I have also begun to dream and dreaming is a big part of listening and discerning God's call in each of our lives.

I rolled her question around in my mind, "What makes you happy?" The visions of my childhood began to swim by in colorful and dancing bubbles, rising up in my thoughts and popping just in time to give me a glimpse of what my bones and blood consider images of happiness: swinging on the tire swing in my grandmother's backyard, the sound of the play by play of the local high school football team echoing through my neighborhood on the autumn Friday nights of my youth, making mixtapes for friends that always held secret meanings—hidden and woven in the lyrics of each song, fire pits and guitars, skipping class to hang out with my friends on Daisy Hill, the rush of possibility when a crush lingers a little longer in a goodbye hug, leaving the first footprints at dawn while walking on the beach, knowing that even in silence and stillness, there is always prayer, reading the vows I would soon take as part of the preparation and prayer practice leading up to my ordination as a deacon, a priest, and becoming a wife. Oh so many times has my heart known and experienced the word happy.

I took another sip of wine, let the berry linger on my tongue before I swallowed. We were there celebrating my birthday. I was now sitting squarely in my mid-forties. I imagined my life so many times as a kid, benchmarking where my parents were at this age and understanding that they are not me and I am not them—our lives have been very different, and yet, filled with happiness, discernment, grief, and prayer. I never could have dreamed this life as a child and yet, when I consider who I am, who I am becoming, the roads I have taken, the roads I did U-turns on, the times I stuck my fingers in both ears and pretended I couldn't hear that still small voice so loud and clear—I hear you now. I feel you now. I am following you now. There will be sadness, yes—but there will be joy, I trust this enough to surrender to you, God. I trust this enough.

My friend gave the space and room I needed to answer her question, the question of what makes me happy.

What makes you happy?

I replied, "Nothing makes me happy. I think life is filled with moments and opportunities that we get to experience and in those moments we get to be happy. We get to be happy. I am happy here, now, with you and I will remember this moment as long as I am able to."

We've played the "What if" game quite a bit lately. She is my beloved, my companion, my wife and she is also my co-dreamer as we listen for God, to God. The wonder and what if of discernment can be overwhelming sometimes, like when you are out hiking and the trail just keeps going up and up and up. I trust that the view will be worth it but sometimes my whole body just needs to stop, rest, pause until ready and then I just keep going. We have started each morning since this time of discernment began with a simple conversation. In this conversation we both surrender to the mystery of what might be and I am grateful that she is the one I get to travel with on this spiritual journey.

I don't know.
You don't know.
God knows.
And that is enough.

What makes you happy? Being in this moment with you and surrendering that God knows, and that is enough.

RECONCILING

We have breathed, remembered, prayed, and released which brings us to another stop in our journey together—reconciling.

The topic of reconciling, from a religious perspective, can be a tricky subject to explore. Reconciliation begins when one accepts that he or she has been missing the mark, or sinning, and the path between our hearts and the heart of our God needs to be unburdened and restored. There are global sins like racism, sexism, homophobia, and extremism in all manner of ways in which we are active or passive players, and then there are sins that are more personal and local to our own hearts. Before I can go on any further I need for us to be on the same page: we are all sinners. I know, no one likes to be called a sinner, but if we can just go ahead and say, "Yes. It is true. I'm not perfect and I am a sinner." Once we can agree on that truth we can move forward towards reconciliation—returning to right relationship with God.

When I came back to the church after being gone for about a dozen years, I realized that what kept me away during the latter part of my journey through the wilderness was the understanding that reconciliation was possible, but it was going to take a period of not only confessing my own sins but being willing to believe that in the heart of our God my sins were already forgiven. The reality wasn't on God to forgive me, but on me to believe that God wiped the slate clean, making my journey home all clear.

In the Book of Common Prayer (used in the Episcopal Church) there is a pastoral office called the Reconciliation of a Penitent (a person who is ready to confess and atone and make amends) that begins this way:

> Have mercy on me, O God, according to your loving-kindness;
> > in your great compassion blot out my offenses.
> Wash me through and through from my wickedness,
> > and cleanse me from my sin.
> For I know my transgressions only too well,
> > and my sin is ever before me.
>
> Holy God, Holy and Mighty, Holy Immortal One,
> > have mercy upon us.
>
> Pray for me, a sinner. (BCP, 449)

The order of this pastoral office continues: the penitent confesses specifically his or her sins, is given the opportunity to forgive others who have sinned against him or her, and concludes with an absolution by the priest. As I stated previously, the harder work, at least for me, began after the final amen of this pastoral office. I needed to settle into the idea and understanding that God had, indeed, forgiven me. As part of my own atonement, and as a way to stay connected to the idea that God does and has and will always forgive us, I feel that it was important to claim my identity as both a sinner and a forgiven child of God.

I spent so many years hiding from my calling to serve God in any capacity because I had this weight of brokenness and sinfulness wrapped around my heart. It took months for me to finally believe, truly, that my sins were blotted out and that the door was open for me to come home; all I needed to do was walk in, and walk in again, and walk in over and over and over until the walk was actually liberation in physical form. It was the hardest walk I have ever ventured on, once a week on Sunday mornings, bringing my brokenness and my hopefulness with me in tow, keeping me company in the liturgy. What has been life-giving is that God has continued to use my brokenness as a place to break into the world in my own spiritual journey. That in-breaking has shaped me and formed me as a Child of God and has allowed me to see where God is already at work in my own ongoing healing process.

What follows in this section are several sermons delivered in times of great dis-ease in our community and in our country. These sermons call out the universal sin that we are participants either willingly or unwillingly. In order to repent for these sins done, left undone, or done on our behalf, we have to acknowledge them, find our fingerprints in the injustice, repent and atone for the wrong we have witnessed. Once we can see our fingerprints in the global context, we know where to begin in our own reconciling of our hearts with God's heart.

Preparing the Way of the Lord

There was a man sent from God, whose name was John. He came as a witness to testify to the light, so that all might believe through him. He himself was not the light, but he came to testify to the light. . . .

This is the testimony given by John when the Jews sent priests and Levites from Jerusalem to ask him, "Who are you?" He confessed and did not deny it, but confessed, "I am not the Messiah." And they asked him, "What then? Are you Elijah?" He said, "I am not." "Are you the prophet?" He answered, "No." Then they said to him, "Who are you? Let us have an answer for those who sent us. What do you say about yourself?" He said,

"I am the voice of one crying out in the wilderness,
'Make straight the way of the Lord,'"
as the prophet Isaiah said.

Now they had been sent from the Pharisees. They asked him, "Why then are you baptizing if you are neither the Messiah, nor Elijah, nor the prophet?" John answered them, "I baptize with water. Among you stands one whom you do not know, the one who is coming after me; I am not worthy to untie the thong of his sandal." This took place in Bethany across the Jordan where John was baptizing. (John 1:6–8, 19–28)

When I was a kid, like a really young kid, I remember going to the Laundromat to do laundry with my mother and younger brother. It wasn't a regular occurrence, so I think we were either between houses or our washing machine at home was on the fritz.

You know kids—they absolutely love to explore and most kids have very few filters, if any. What they are thinking is what they are saying. My younger brother is a case in point. We were there, putting clothes into the washers, and then from the washers into the dryers—taking in the noise from the one TV sitting bolted to the table that was bolted to the floor; seeing the flashing lights from the video games; hearing the chatter of other mothers and children, men and older men—so much happening at one time. Each breath was filled with a floral cotton scent: that warm smell of dryers tumbling and tumbling. Above the chatter and the sound of drums turning, my brother asked my mother, "Why are there so many brown people here?" He was three or four at the time.

The look in my mother's eyes is something that has stuck with me. Her eyes expressed both love and another emotion I didn't fully understand then. He was right: there was a bunch of brown people there. In our world, we knew two brown people—one being our across the street neighbor who had a panache for being grandmotherly and otherworldly at the same time. The other brown person in our lives was an elderly woman who was a part of my mom's upbringing.

Yes, the public schools were desegregated, but we attended a private school for pre-K and Kindergarten. Our school experience was blissfully and southernly white. So to be in the mix, in community with brown people, even if it was for just the time needed to wash, dry, and fold laundry, seemed out of the ordinary and my younger brother was just making that observation.

When I was in second grade I remember telling a joke to my friends at recess that I read in a book called *Truly Tasteless Jokes: Volume 3*. I'm not going to tell the joke now because I remember the reaction I got from my circle of friends. It was—as I have now come to understand—a racist joke. There are very few moments in my life that I truly, in the depth of my soul, regret. This would be one of them. I told a racist joke, at the age of nine, not knowing why some of my friends would be offended.

Why am I saying any of this? Because we are living in a time that beckons each of us to understand ourselves better in order to make sense of what is happening in our world today. Michael Brown, Eric Garner, Trayvon Martin, John Crawford, Armand Bennet, Ezell Ford, Jeremy Lake: these are the names of people who are brown, black; who have been killed, lost forever. We are left without knowing what their impact in life would have been on each of us, and we are left to carry on, to seek deeper understanding that begins by seeking why some of us will never ever have to question if our very presence—in a store, a restaurant, a public place—will raise suspicion from other people in positions of power.

Many may feel that these issues were dealt with by the likes of Martin Luther King Jr., Rosa Parks, Vernon Johns, Adam Clayton Powell Jr., Percy Julian. and on and on and on . . . but look around: racism is rearing its head and the price is high, and the cost will only go up—with interest—until we take an honest, long, hard look in the mirror and estimate what we have contributed to the equation.

I did that this week. I did this a couple of weeks ago. And the truth is I can't fully understand what it is like to be not white in this country. I can't. That is not my option, my ability; but I also can't let myself off the hook because I'm white.

Black lives matter. I can say that with authority because in my baptism and confirmation and my desire to follow the path of Jesus Christ I am led to believe that all are precious in the sight of God. But if I say that black lives matter without taking the time to do a full inventory of my own life, I become just another talking head talking on the topic of the moment, saying what is supposed to be said and then moving on. Moving on without taking the time to really get to know why just saying black lives matter makes me uncomfortable.

I used to say I was colorblind until a friend of mine told me that was a cop-out. He said, by saying I was colorblind I was removing the experience people of color lived through on a daily basis. He said, "You can't discount my very existence by saying that my skin color doesn't matter, because it does.

And yours does too. The way the world perceives you and me, whether we like it or not, takes into account the color of our skin."

I have wrestled long and hard with what I should say or do in response to Ferguson, New York, Florida, Ohio, Wilmington, Baltimore, Charlotte, and other places where people of color have had to be more alert of their surroundings based solely on the color of their skin. And the truth is, there is no one golden answer but there is a call for us, each of us, to get to know ourselves better in order to offer the world a response that comes from that place of knowing: not just repeating the catch phrase, black lives matter, but knowing why we think, say, and believe, indeed, that black lives matter.

It starts by knowing ourselves. It starts by telling our own stories regarding race, our own biasness. It starts by sitting in the middle of our discomfort and not running from, discounting, or absolving our discomfort, but acknowledging that something about this real and honest conversation causes our foundation to become shaken. We begin to examine our hearts around the subject of racism when we see that the precedents our country is based on have historically regarded positions of power and authority as being offered to those with white skin. It starts by understanding how our presence affects the world around us, and also knowing that all of what we have experienced affects the words we say, the way we hold ourselves, the way the world perceives us. And knowing that before we ever say one word we are being judged and we are judging. But our responsibility doesn't end there. Our responsibility is to say, "Okay, I've taken the time to delve deeper. Now how can I use my position and experience to make the future better? Hell, to make the present better?"

John the Baptist was out there, down by the river, greeting everyone who made the hard, uncomfortable, and sometimes dangerous journey through the wilderness of uncertainty and doubt and remorse. He would dunk anyone who showed up ready to repent for their sins, whether they fully understood those sins or not. He was out there telling anyone and everyone that things could change, that things would change, but they had to risk. We have to risk being honest. We have to say that what we have been doing isn't working, and we have to invite God into the conversation by acknowledging we can't do this on our own.

Prepare the way of the Lord.

One way we can prepare the way of the Lord is to search our hearts, our history and truly look at the fingerprints we have left on the struggle for equality, respect, and the living out of our baptismal covenant.

Prepare the way of the Lord: get to know who you are, whom God has created you to be; admit that you have fallen way short of the bar set by God; admit how you truly are on Monday, Tuesday, Wednesday, Thursday, Friday, and Saturday.

Prepare the way of the Lord. No one is perfect. We can either flip the channels and repeat popular slogans without doing the work to fully embrace the words we are saying, or we can—in our discomfort—make ourselves feel better by dragging our own biasness into the equation.

My friends, there is much to be done. There are grieving families who have lost sons, hopes; they have lost the American dream. Even if Eric or Michael or Trayvon were participating in law-breaking behaviors, when did that become grounds for being eradicated?

Prepare the way of the Lord.

Prepare the way of the Lord.

Find a way to convert your words into action. Find the courage to sit within your own discomfort and understand where the root of your discomfort, our discomfort comes from.

Prepare the way of the Lord. If we are doing it right, people are going to try and shut us down, shut us out, question our authority, invalidate our role. Don't shy away from those moments when you are scared. Instead, invite God into that place. God understands, fully, the price of losing a brown-skinned son, a loved one, and yet God still finds the grace and mercy to continue to love those who held some sort of responsibility for that son's death.

The solution begins when we each take a moment to understand our own story. Just as we can't get to Christmas without heeding the words of John to prepare the way of the Lord, we can't get to full equality without understanding our own place, our role in that dance.

Prepare the way of the Lord, even when the work is hard and uncomfortable.

Amen.

Grace and the Nameless Woman

One of the Pharisees asked Jesus to eat with him, and he went into the Pharisee's house and took his place at the table. And a woman in the city, who was a sinner, having learned that he was eating in the Pharisee's house, brought an alabaster jar of ointment. She stood behind him at his feet, weeping, and began to bathe his feet with her tears and to dry them with her hair. Then she continued kissing his feet and anointing them with the ointment. Now when the Pharisee who had invited him saw it, he said to himself, "If this man were a prophet, he would have known who and what kind of woman this is who is touching him—that she is a sinner." Jesus spoke up and said to him, "Simon, I have something to say to you." "Teacher," he replied, "Speak." "A certain creditor had two debtors; one owed five hundred denarii, and the other fifty. When they could not pay, he canceled the debts for both of them. Now which of them will love him more?" Simon answered, "I suppose the one for whom he canceled the greater debt." And Jesus said to him, "You have judged rightly." Then turning toward the woman, he said to Simon, "Do you see this woman? I entered your house; you gave me no water for my feet, but she has bathed my feet with her tears and dried them with her hair. You gave me no kiss, but from the time I came in she has not stopped kissing my feet. You did not anoint my head with oil, but she has anointed my feet with ointment. Therefore, I tell you, her sins, which were many, have been forgiven; hence she has shown great love. But the one to whom little is forgiven, loves little." Then he said to her, "Your sins are forgiven." But those who were at the table with him began to say among themselves, "Who is this who even forgives sins?" And he said to the woman, "Your faith has saved you; go in peace."

Soon afterwards he went on through cities and villages, proclaiming and bringing the good news of the kingdom of God. The twelve were with him, as well as some women who had been cured of evil spirits and infirmities: Mary, called Magdalene, from whom seven demons had gone out, and Joanna, the wife of Herod's steward Chuza, and Susanna, and many others, who provided for them out of their resources. (Luke 7:36–8:3)

I read this gospel passage last Sunday evening, which is what I do every Sunday evening. I end a day of worship by beginning to prepare for the following week's worship. I like to read and then let it stew for a couple of days before trying to formulate my ideas into a sermon. I like to read the gospel and then look at the world around me: listen to what is making news, observe the rhythm of the heartbeat in these streets. Then—maybe—I can cull together an idea that is worth listening to on a Sunday morning. That's how it goes most weeks.

But this week was different. I was physically made to feel discomfort when I read this gospel passage. I've never been comfortable with public displays of affection, and this unnamed woman pushed that button hard within me. Who would do such a thing? Who would walk in uninvited, risk life and freedom to touch a stranger in such a way, and bend down and kiss his dirty feet and then bathe them in tears and ointment? Who would do such a thing? The answer that I keep coming back to is this: a person who has nothing left to lose.

Her story is echoed in one way or another in all four gospels. She is nameless in Luke's version of the gospel. We don't know where she is from. We don't know her name. We don't know much about her at all except that she is a sinner: a sinful woman, a sinful soul. And she has nothing left to lose. So why not go big? Why not atone for her sin in a grand gesture? People were already talking about her behind her back, covering their mouths and whispering when they saw her on the street, already teaching their sons not to fall for women like her, teaching their daughters to mind their "P"s and "Q"s in order to not become her. There was nothing this woman could do that would make their whispers and judgments stop. She would forever be known in her community as the nameless sinful woman. That's the way we know her in the gospel account. She doesn't even have a name to lose. She has nothing. Nothing left to lose.

On Monday, I read an article about another woman who had nothing left to lose. She lost her safety, security, and the comfort of being in her own skin through an unwanted, unasked for, assault on her body. After the names this woman has been called, the doubt and judgment cast upon her, the daily mountains she has to climb just to get out of bed, the realization that part of her name will always be the one who got raped behind a dumpster: she had nothing left to lose, so she asked the judge if she could address her attacker directly at the sentencing hearing. There, in the middle of the room, this woman walked in and did something that made everyone uncomfortable. She broke open the alabaster jar of ointment that filled the room up with its perfume. She washed the room over and over with her tears and her story. She let her hair hang in a tangled mass, messy and unkempt. Filled with pain and hurt and trauma, she held up a mirror within her words, played back the questions she was asked, told her part of the story, and told him exactly what he had done to her. Even with the framing and reframing of violation, the account of her sexual assault has resulted in Pharisees and judges telling people under their breath that she is a very sinful woman. The weight of the life she has to live with daily has caused her posture to change and change again. Many people have blamed her. Many people still do, saying it's her fault that she was raped, much like those in Simon's dining room who said, "If Jesus were a prophet, he would have known who and what kind of woman this is who is touching him—that she is a sinner." The judge in her rape case seems to have agreed and gave her attacker a sentence of six months in the county jail, reduced it to three months and once those three months were over, he returned to a life of freedom.

But Jesus changes the narrative. The grace that Jesus pours out for the sinful woman is poured out for each of us—for all of us—regardless of the tally of sins we carry in our hearts, on our skin, or in our scars and wounds. Jesus doesn't keep score; Jesus has more important things to do when it comes to being our Savior and Messiah. And Jesus asks us to do the same for one another . . . every day. Because he has forgiven us, we must in turn forgive each other. I believe in the very marrow of my bones that this is the hardest part of following Jesus, of walking with others in the Jesus movement. Sin and forgiveness comes with the job. Not one of us lives a life so holy that we don't find ourselves in need of grace and forgiveness. And because any one of us could have been that nameless woman in the gospel story, we need to examine how we sometimes, maybe—just maybe, use another's life and sins as a measuring stick against our own. The truth is, God's grace is not a commodity to be traded and measured out. God's grace is given, no questions asked and nothing is needed in exchange.

Such is the grace the nameless woman received. She went from being nameless and sinful to nameless and forgiven, just like that. Her story was forever changed. Her life would never be the same.

Simon's life was also forever changed, if he was brave enough to admit that in Jesus's eyes, he and the woman were equal—in sinfulness and in receiving God's grace and forgiveness. That was up to Simon. That is up to each of us. The Kingdom of God is a place of great equality where we don't dwell on our past, the forgiveness and grace given to each of us through Jesus Christ. We have much to do and learn to bring about the Kingdom of God in our time and in our place. When we walk through the doors here at Trinity, there is a place for you here, in the space. When we offer up the prayers of the people, we are praying for all the souls gathered in this room. When we pray the confession and absolution is given, it is given without any strings attached, the same way Jesus absolves us before we even say a word. When we pass the peace to one another, that peace is the peace of Christ that is given freely to all, a gift for us to hold onto on Monday, Tuesday, Wednesday. It gives us the courage to speak our truth and address those who shake our own sense of peace. It wraps around us to comfort us when our child is missing. It is what we offer to each other in the darkness of our fears. When we arrive at communion we hear the words, "He stretched out his arms upon the cross, and offered himself, in obedience to your will, a perfect sacrifice for the whole world." For the whole world. No caveats, no asterisks, no ifs, ands, or buts. The whole world. Even nameless sinful women. Even named, self-important Pharisees.

If the Pharisee Simon had his way, that would not be the case. But let us also remember that Christ was kind enough to point out the differences between this nameless woman and Simon: "I entered your house; you gave me no water for my feet, but she has bathed my feet with her tears and dried them with her hair. You gave me no kiss, but from the time I came in she has not stopped kissing my feet. You did not anoint my head with oil, but she has anointed my feet with ointment. Therefore, I tell you, her sins, which were many, have been forgiven; hence she has shown great love. But the one to whom little is forgiven, loves little" (Luke 7:44–47).

When a person enters into our house—as a guest, as a visitor, as a person who just needs a place to sit and rest, as a new member, as a longtime member, as a prodigal son or daughter—let us greet them with the hospitality fit for Christ. We are one community: flawed, sinful, blemished, beautiful, beloved by God, forgiven by Christ, and drenched in grace—a human family. Sometimes we just need to be made uncomfortable, stirred out of our comfort zones to remember that brokenness and sinfulness is a part of our story but so is reconciliation. Amen.

A Reflection on the Pulse Massacre

Now before faith came, we were imprisoned and guarded under the law until faith would be revealed. Therefore the law was our disciplinarian until Christ came, so that we might be justified by faith. But now that faith has come, we are no longer subject to a disciplinarian, for in Christ Jesus you are all children of God through faith. As many of you as were baptized into Christ have clothed yourselves with Christ. There is no longer Jew or Greek, there is no longer slave or free, there is no longer male and female; for all of you are one in Christ Jesus. And if you belong to Christ, then you are Abraham's offspring, heirs according to the promise. (Galatians 3:23–29)

It was early on a Sunday morning when I saw the headline, "Gay nightclub comes under attack." I thought perhaps Westboro Baptist Church was out protesting again. Oh, what I would have given for that to have been the case. The gay community knows how to deal with protestors. I read on to find that a gunman had gone into a gay club in Orlando and fired into the crowd on purpose. The club posted to its Facebook page, encouraging people to run out the door and keep running. I will admit that I originally thought it was a funny way of announcing closing time. But there was nothing funny about what happened in that club.

I went to church to open up the building and set up communion for the 8:00 a.m. service without knowing many details about the shooting. I checked my voicemail and e-mail, ran through my sermon once or twice, and had a few minutes to hop online. Twenty dead: that was the number known at 7:40 a.m. Twenty dead. I was speechless. We have to pray, I thought. We will add this to the prayers of the people.

We worshipped, had coffee hour, worshipped again, had another coffee hour. I got home just before 1:00 p.m. and remarked to my wife, "Can you believe he killed twenty people?"

"Fifty," she replied.

"No. Twenty," I countered.

"Fifty," Barbie said again, and I felt like I had been punched in the gut, knocked out of breath. I felt numb and scared.

Why? One death is too many, and I had just begun to wrap my head around twenty. But fifty? The heartache and pain were unbearable. I sat in my kitchen for the rest of the day trying really hard not to move. I can't explain why except I didn't feel safe, so I was trying to take up as little space as possible. Anger came next. Anger at expressions of "our thoughts and prayers are with the victims and their families." I was jaded and cynical about that expression. I wanted to see a new phrase attached to the current trend of thoughts and prayers: ". . . and this is what I am doing to change the story. To change the refrain. To change the world we live in." But to only say we are thinking and praying for the victims without any kind of action to remedy the situation was wasted time and wasted breath because the world shouts back, "Keep your prayers, we don't want them."

A friend who has known me for years heard my anger and wrote, "Ginny, prayers are important. For some it is just the beginning. For others, it is all they have to give." I felt pretty small in that moment. And I realized I had to figure out how to preach in the weeks to come, when all I felt like I could say was, "How long, Oh Lord, must we wait? Come Holy Spirit, come."

That afternoon I read the passage for the following Sunday and my heart was moved by Paul's words to the Galatians, particularly verse 3:28: "There is no longer Jew or Greek, there is no longer slave or free, there is no longer male and female; for all of you are one in Christ Jesus." I needed to hear those words. I needed to read them, mark them, inwardly digest them, and write them on my hands and on my heart.

I don't know if you have ever had the chance to go dancing at a self-identified gay bar. There is real freedom in those clubs. No one cares if you are gay or straight or somewhere in between. No one cares if you are black or white or Hispanic or Native American or Asian. No one asks if you are Butch, femm, masculine, a drag queen or king, Christian, Jewish, Muslim, agnostic, or atheist. All they care about is that you, as a patron, are kind, considerate, pay your tab, and will call a cab if you need help getting home.

I loved my nights dancing. I loved them and I learned through them. I figured out how to be a part of a community through them—a community that struggled for generations for freedom, for safety, for help in the AIDS crisis; a community that celebrated milestones in achievements while advancing our causes and cries for respect and dignity and safety. This community knew how to celebrate and be brave and bold. No matter who you were, you were welcome and accepted once you got through the doors, paid your cover, and walked on the dance floor.

Later that Sunday evening, after I had had a chance to catch my breath and wake up a bit from the desire to stay as still as possible, I found my anger still present and, at times, overwhelming. I sensed within me a deep desire to confess and repent and try again.

The shooter was Muslim. Yes. But I couldn't automatically hate every single Muslim because of this one guy's actions. Most Muslims were just as upset about the tragedy as I was. They did not condone it. Our Muslim brothers and sisters in Wilmington, where I live, spoke up. Muslims showed up at the blood banks in Orlando with fruit and water to hand out to people waiting to give blood, even though it was in the holy month of Ramadan when they cannot eat or drink from sunup to sundown. They gave what they could and offered support, even as they condemned the attack.

We live in a time where we are constantly being put into either/or categories. These categories have become more and more divisive and harmful. Here are just a few examples: White or person of color; Christian or some other religion; employed or too lazy to work; men or mothers, providers or absent fathers (unless of course you can't or don't want children—then there is a whole other word for people like us). And that is just the beginning. As long as we allow ourselves to be put into categories that demonize one another, we will never come close to knowing the true peace of Christ or the Kingdom of God. We too often perpetuate images put forth by the media in our own communities and conversations. And we say it and say it and say it until it becomes a part of our narrative.

And we say it and say it and say it until it becomes a part of our narrative and then it becomes truth and then it becomes fact.

Paul, in his letter to the Galatians, was trying desperately to get the attention of the church—that this need to categorize and demonize and create a hierarchical system was not going to aid them in following Christ and would actually do more harm. I think Paul is preaching to us again, through history and through love—it is time to see the other in only one light—as family. It shouldn't matter if the other believes in Christ, it is enough if we do. And it is through the love of Christ that we need to work on letting go of the categories and hold onto being one, in Christ Jesus. May the souls of the departed rest in peace and rise in glory, and may God protect us, all of us, and hold us accountable to do the same.

Amen.

A Lost Sheep

At that time the festival of the Dedication took place in Jerusalem. It was winter, and Jesus was walking in the temple, in the portico of Solomon. So the Jews gathered around him and said to him, "How long will you keep us in suspense? If you are the Messiah, tell us plainly." Jesus answered, "I have told you, and you do not believe. The works that I do in my Father's name testify to me; but you do not believe, because you do not belong to my sheep. My sheep hear my voice. I know them, and they follow me. I give them eternal life, and they will never perish. No one will snatch them out of my hand. What my Father has given me is greater than all else, and no one can snatch it out of the Father's hand. The Father and I are one." (John 10:22–30)

I am the good shepherd.

There was a time in my life when I thought the flock was off limits to me. I thought I didn't make the cut, that my blemishes were just a bit too extravagant and just a bit too much for the flock to handle. I thought that my approach to the world and my approach to God didn't quite gel with the ways and means of the flock. It wasn't just me thinking this. Other sheep came up to me and said, "Unwelcomed," "Not wanted," "Get away from here."

But others from the flock said, "Sure, come on in and join us," so I did. I came into the flock, sat down, and ate with them. Yet before I could even swallow my first bit of food, they were already telling me what I needed to change in order to fit in. Everything they wanted to change was external, but my longing to be in the flock was internal. My need to be connected to the shepherd was soulful and heartfelt. It wasn't until they wanted me to change part of my soul and heart that I realized this flock was not a safe place for me. So I left.

And I wandered.

And I was lonely.

And I was empty.

And then I became angry. Angry at the flock. Then my anger turned to bitterness and it got real close to touching hate—real close but it never crossed that line.

I walked around the pastures, taking in the beauty. I sniffed the wind, watched the clouds' shape shift in the sky. I huddled near rocks and stones when the rains fell or when the snow drifted. It wasn't so bad, but at night when the moon would rise and the stars would wink and drift and fall and blaze, I really felt homesick. Flock-sick. I felt incomplete. Just over the peak of the hill I could hear the flock resting together, eating together, playing together. I could hear the shepherd's voice calling to his sheep. I felt the pull on my own heart: it was beautiful and painful; peaceful and painful; hopeful and painful—because it was made clear to me that I didn't belong. Painfully clear: I didn't belong.

I drifted for a bit and found ways to fill that emptiness. I made sure I kept busy. I drowned out the shepherd's voice with music, with work, with relationships, with exhaustion, with school: anything I could do that would stave off the loneliness and that would feel somewhat meaningful.

I found a group of others who felt unwanted and together we made our own flock. It felt good to belong, to be a part of something, to be seen and heard and understood. We would sit around, talk about stuff, celebrate each other in our good times, and cry together in our bad times. We drank. Lord, did we drink. And we partied. Good Lord, did we party. We laughed until we cried, and then we cried until we laughed. We lived together, we played together, we ate together and I thought, "This is good." And it was. It was the closest thing to a flock I knew. But there was no shepherd. No one looking out for us. No one able or ready to pull us back when we got too close to the edge. No one ready or able to come look for us when we got lost. And we were forever getting lost. We let each other do our own things and sometimes that meant leaving the flock we had put together. No one batted an eye.

What we had were cell phones. And the internet. We had Bloody Mary bars with all the fixings. We had dance floors and late nights. We had girlfriends, boyfriends, crushes, and exes. We had jobs and school and bills. We had plans and dreams, but most of them centered on next weekend; not many of them included any other lost sheep, or taking care of any needs other than our own. This makeshift flock was unsustainable. The more I thought about it, the more I realized we were a party, not a flock. We had no shepherd. No one at the table ever mentioned the shepherd. If, by chance, he came up, the person was shamed into silence and their loyalty was questioned.

"We don't need a shepherd. We are doing just fine on our own."

I left that flock. I left them. I still love them, but I just couldn't let go of the idea that I do, in fact, need a shepherd. But where was I going to find a flock that had a good shepherd and that wouldn't ask me to change part of myself in order to be a part of that flock?

"My sheep hear my voice. I know them, and they follow me."

The shepherd found me and called me as I was driving my 2000 Ford Focus up I-95 from Florida back to North Carolina. I took my girlfriend on a surprise trip to Disney World where she surprised me by saying, "I love you, but I'm not in love with you and I don't see this going anywhere." Surprise!

The Good Shepherd whispered my name and said, "It's time. It's time to come home."

I wrestled with him saying, "Yeah, but I have tried and your flock is mean and judgmental and I don't want to be part of them."

"Trust me," the shepherd said. "Those sheep—the ones that hurt you and harmed you and caused you to stray. I've been working on them just as I have been working on you. Some have left because they don't believe me when I say that my love is offered freely for all. They didn't belong because they didn't believe that God chooses ALL over some every time, that God chooses love over hate every time, that God chooses compassion over cantankerousness every time, that God sends me to you, to find you and to bring you back, every time.

"Every time. When a person is able to see and believe that my love is for them and for their neighbors—no exceptions, no caveats—then they understand that they belong. Sometimes this kind of love is too much for a person to comprehend, but the gate is open and all are welcome to belong and believe. You hear my voice and you know my voice. Let me shepherd you. Let me bring you home again. Come and follow me."

I stood on the steps of a church I had passed by every single day for four years. I stood on those steps summoning up the courage to take the hardest first steps in my life; 99.9% of me wanted to turn tail and head home, but somehow I made it through the door and into a pew where I was greeted and welcomed and invited.

"Oh, you have blemishes, I have blemishes. You have matts in your coat. Me, too. You have scars. I have scars. No one is perfect. Here is a bulletin. Do you have any questions? We have questions too. Don't worry about the doubts, we all have those too. We are just so glad you are here." That is how the conversation went once I got into the building. I wasn't asked to prove that I was worthy. I didn't have to change anything in order to stay. I just needed to open my heart a little wider and trust that the Good Shepherd wouldn't lead me astray.

That is a heavy burden you are carrying. Here, set that down. You are absolved.

You must be starving. Here is some bread and some wine. There is enough for everyone regardless of how long it has been.

Let us pray for our own needs and the needs of others. I prayed among the flock, in the body of Christ, connected to the other sheep around me. I prayed for forgiveness. I prayed for reconciliation. I prayed for my friends out there who were as lost as I was. I prayed for the sheep that struggled to believe that Jesus's love was meant for every single sheep. No questions, no exceptions. I prayed and thanked God for the courage to try again and for the grace of the Good Shepherd guiding me home.

For whatever reason, your journey brought you here, to this day, to this moment, and somehow this moment has found you reading about a lost sheep. Whether you identify as a lost sheep or as something else, rest assured, you are not alone. There are many of us in various stages of our spiritual journey. We are loved beyond measure, even when we don't understand why or how. The Good Shepherd is seeking you, being sent out to find you and to bring you back from wherever you may be. The journey home is filled with all kinds of feelings, but it begins by surrendering, breathing, remembering, praying, releasing, and reconciling. When we return home led by the Good Shepherd, we are reunited with the flock, fed with abundance, blessed, forgiven, and sent back out—but not alone; rather, connected to the something greater that our hearts long to find. This homecoming is our touching place, a place to connect and rejuvenate us. The shepherd has led each of us here, but there are others out there who are just as lost and just as hungry. Perhaps, and I know this is pretty radical stuff, but perhaps they are waiting or needing an invitation to come and try again or try for the first time, to see if this part of the flock is where they need to be. It doesn't hurt to ask and it just might be a saving grace for a sheep. I know it was for me.

I once was lost but now I'm found was blind but now I'm a sheep.

Amen.

The King of Second Chances

When they came to the place that is called The Skull, they crucified Jesus there with the criminals, one on his right and one on his left. Then Jesus said, "Father, forgive them; for they do not know what they are doing." And they cast lots to divide his clothing. The people stood by, watching Jesus on the cross; but the leaders scoffed at him, saying, "He saved others; let him save himself if he is the Messiah of God, his chosen one!" The soldiers also mocked him, coming up and offering him sour wine, and saying, "If you are the King of the Jews, save yourself!" There was also an inscription over him, "This is the King of the Jews."

One of the criminals who were hanged there kept deriding him and saying, "Are you not the Messiah? Save yourself and us!" But the other rebuked him, saying, "Do you not fear God, since you are under the same sentence of condemnation? And we indeed have been condemned justly, for we are getting what we deserve for our deeds, but this man has done nothing wrong." Then he said, "Jesus, remember me when you come into your kingdom." He replied, "Truly I tell you, today you will be with me in Paradise." (Luke 23:33–43)

This story began long before the morning of this day, this fateful day. The story began years ago at his birth. Actually, the story began before that too. He was a poor son born into a poor family. He was the first-born; that placement in the structure of his family came with many benefits but also with many payments. His parents were new to parenting. Sometimes they were overprotective and sometimes they just didn't know what to do. There were other family members, other arms that held, other hearts that taught him, other souls that would be there for him in the darkest of days.

His father woke up every morning before the sun, before the heat of the day, before the birds preened the sleep from their feathers and gathered his tools, his sandals, and a bit of lunch and headed out to work. This was the work his father taught him and his father's father taught him and this is the work he would one day learn and then in turn teach his son.

But what if I don't like it?

But what if I am no good at it?

But what if I want to do something else?

Although these questions visited him as he approached the year he would begin his apprenticeship with his father, he never voiced them—he knew better. Unless he was promised to the temple, to the synagogue, there was no escaping his destiny. No escape. Those are the words that haunted him. Those are the words every teenager runs from no matter what year they were born and what the customs were of the day—no escape. No escape. No escape. Until one surrenders and understands the Holy Truth: Thy will be done.

He never intended to end up here. He never intended to have the final days of his life put on display for the entire world to see and to mock and to jeer at his most unfortunate predicament. As he looks out from his perch, he sees the morning dew burning off the scattered foliage causing an eerie haze. It's going to be a hot day today, he thinks to himself. A hot day. Nothing I can do about it. Guess I will have to sweat.

In the pause between inhaling and exhaling, his mind flashes back to a time when he was sixteen—which really wasn't that long ago. He sees himself in his tunic and sandals hanging out with a couple of friends—friends he had known for most of his life. They were talking about girls and jobs and the upcoming marriage of one of them. Feeling a little less than in the conversation, like his life isn't interesting or exciting enough, he decided to boast that he could steal and not get caught. He didn't realize that he was opening up an invitation from his friends to prove that statement. After a few minutes of chiding and razzing, his boasting was put to the test—the object of the engagement: to steal fruit from a vendor's cart without being caught.

"Why am I doing this?" kept running through his thoughts as he approached the cart. "You don't have to do this," another statement answered back. "But they will laugh at me if I don't. They will taunt me. They might even disown me as their friend." He approached the cart, nervously palmed a piece of fruit, and tucked it into his sleeve and quickly walked away . . . until he felt the strong hand of the vendor grabbing the back of his tunic.

Cold fear ran through his body. The kind of adrenaline rush that makes your heart both race and stop at the same time. As the vendor jerked him back, he could hear the laughter of his friends roaring in the background. They laughed at me anyway, he thought. The fruit rolled out of his sleeve, hit the ground with a thud, and came to rest about three feet away from him.

"I caught you, you little thief," the vendor said with a fixed jaw and rage in his eyes. "You think you can steal from me? I know you. I know your father. What's going to happen to you when I tell him you tried to rob me?"

"Please sir, don't tell him. I am sorry."

His friends' laugher grew more as tears filled his eyes and he began to cry. They were taunting him behind the vendor's back, making cry-baby motions with their fists to their eyes. I really blew this, he thought to himself. To God.

The world around him got still, and everything faded away, the only thing he could see was the vendor in front of him, the baskets of fruit—so beautiful in their shape and color, and all he could say was, "No escape, no escape, no escape—thy will be done."

Which shocked the vendor, and rightly so. In that moment of surrendering, the vendor let go of the sleeve of the teenager and said, "Here, take this too," and he handed the boy another piece of fruit. "Your father and I have been friends for a long time; we got into plenty of trouble together growing up. Take this and give it to your friends but don't, don't do it again, okay?"

And suddenly he is back in this day, caught up in the memory, and he says aloud through parched lips and dry tongue, "Okay."

The sun was higher now. And hotter, much hotter. Perhaps he had dozed off and was just waking up again. Perhaps all of this was a bad dream and any moment now he was going to wake up in his comfortable bed next to his beautiful wife. Perhaps, after getting up, he would sit down to breakfast with his children before collecting his tools and head off to work, just like his father did every day while he was growing up. But he knew better. He knew this was not a dream. The pain in his arms and in his legs and in his heart was too much to bear in a dream.

He looked at the faces of the people gathered, hoping to see one familiar face, one person who knew him and still loved him. No one. No escape, no escape, no escape—thy will be done.

Suffice it to say that the opportunity to take the different path that the vendor offered to him—to never steal again, to never try to be more than who God created him to be—was not an opportunity he took. The very opposite occurred. He never really became a good thief either. Obviously. He got caught. Several times. And finally he was judged and sentenced. At nineteen years old, he was going to be the first of his friends to die.

He mustered a laugh that caused agony to ripple throughout his body. He was in and out of consciousness now. Is this real? Is this a dream?

He did know that he was not alone on the hill. Besides the guards and onlookers, two other men were there with him. He didn't know why one of them was there but he knew the story of the man in the middle. He was called the King of the Jews. The thief had heard stories about this man, stories of his teachings, his miracles, his healings. He had even thought to himself at an earlier day of trying it out—walking with those who followed him, a new life, a new way of living. But that never really materialized for the thief, the leaving behind his old life in order to start again, to start over, to be made new. And even if it had, would following the King of the Jews have spared him from his current situation? Being crucified? Next to the Son of God?

As the young thief was recalling yet another missed opportunity, the man next to him began to speak, not loudly but as if he was having a conversation. He said:

"No escape. No escape. No escape. Thy will be done."

The guards had teased this man, asking him to save himself. Even the man on the other side of us teased him too: "Save yourself, Messiah. Boy king. Save yourself if you really are the Messiah."

Flashbacks to the thief's own group of friends and the ribbing they gave him, egging him on, encouraging him to do acts that would earn their friendship. Why? Why did I do that? Why did I keep doing that?

There had to be something to this man, this Messiah. For even in all the suffering he was enduring on the cross and from what had been told about the trial, this man hadn't been broken; battered, bruised, bloodied, but not broken.

The man in the middle spoke again, this time louder, "Father forgive them, for they do not know what they are doing."

This was meant for the guards, the onlookers. and maybe, just maybe even for himself, the thief, the nineteen-year old son, the never-been-married husband in waiting, the boy who knew forgiveness from a vendor and the pain of laughter of his friends. Forgive me. Forgive me. Forgive me. Thy will be done.

"Jesus, I am so sorry. Remember me when you come into your kingdom."

Jesus said, "I heard you every time you said you were sorry. I heard you every time you wrestled with what you were doing. There is nothing you can do that will make me stop loving you."

That is the kingship of our Lord. That is the kingship of our Lord proclaimed throughout the gospels, lived out in our daily faith. It is good to be reminded that even in his death he had love to share and give; and that love is free, beyond measure or understanding. Even on the Cross—in his last minutes of life among us—he forgave and he loved. He forgave and he loved a thief, the guards, his persecutors then and his persecutors now, those that saw him as a threat; he forgave and he loved. He forgives and he loves us on our good days and on our bad days. When we are awesome at being followers of Christ and when we fall way short in loving God and our neighbors. The kingship of Christ is one rooted and based in second, third, fourth chances. The thief finally got it in that moment. And on this day, this Christ the King Sunday, this last Sunday of our Liturgical year, take some time later to reflect on how your life and spiritual journey has been blessed by the God of Second Chances, by the Christ that is our king.

Forgive me, forgive me, forgive me; thy will be done.

Amen.

Ending to Begin Again

For I am convinced that neither death, nor life, nor angels, nor rulers, nor things present, nor things to come, nor powers, nor height, nor depth, nor anything else in all creation, will be able to separate us from the love of God in Christ Jesus our Lord. (Romans 8:38–39)

Perhaps this is a good place to end or perhaps this is an invitation to begin again.

What I want you to know, more than anything, is that you are a beloved and treasured child of God. The prayers you offer up on behalf of those who are dealing with so much are heard and appreciated. Your heart is a beautiful gift, one that is generous and kind, and the world is a better place because of you. Don't let the darkness of this world damper you or your light. Keep shining, keep praying, keep being the hands, feet, heart, and mind of Christ in this world. You give me hope and strength and encouragement to shine my own light in this life. I give thanks this day for you, for all the gifts you have, and for all the many ways you share those gifts. Do good, love your neighbors, shine your light, and welcome the joy of this life into your life with open arms. If you are struggling, tell someone, and if you come across someone who is struggling, tell them that they matter and that they are worthy of a love that knows no boundaries or barriers. Don't forget to breathe, remember, pray, and release, and through all of that, you are reconciling your heart and the heart of our God. Bless you and the steps you walk today, and may the Peace of Christ be with you and remain with you always, but especially today.

ACKNOWLEDGMENTS

Amazing things can happen when you are given time to dream. I am finding this to be true. What started off as a simple line item in my Big Grand Dream for my first CREDO experience in October 2015 is now a reality: "I want to write a book." I didn't do this on my own, however, and there are some people I would like to thank.

Thank you to Trinity Episcopal Parish in Wilmington, Delaware—the church I have served since graduating from seminary in 2012. You all have been so kind and generous, open and affirming of me and my creative expressions, allowing me to seek and serve God through music, writing, and Bible studies in a bar. God sends us out to do the work and you all have given me permission to do exactly that. Thank you.

Thank you to the Rev. Patricia Downing, my rector and mentor. Your support and your encouragement have helped me so much in my first years as a priest. Thank you for teaching me that the work we are called to do asks us to risk, to be brave, to be bold, and to be the light in our often dark world.

Thank you to my beloved wife, Barbie. Oh, my love. I knew we were in for an adventure from the moment we met, and I can't imagine traveling through this world without you. Thank you for your words of wisdom, your laughter, your encouragement, and for adding so much life and light to my heart. I don't know. You don't know. God knows, and that is enough.

Thank you to community of faith at the Cathedral of All Souls in Asheville, North Carolina. When I was ready to come home, you offered me a place to be still and remember through the liturgy, the hymns, the confession, absolution, peace, and communion, that there is nothing any of us can do that will separate us from the love of our God. Thank you for being a soft place to land.

A final thank you to my grandmother, Effie Leland Wilder, who wrote her first novel at the age of eighty-five. A lifelong lover of music, a prayerful and faithful soul, a woman who loved to tell a story—I see your fingerprints all over my heart, Nana. You taught me that we don't have to agree completely in order to completely love. What I wouldn't give to hear you call me "Doodle" one more time.